SO YOU THINK YOU KNOW SHAKESPEARE?

CLIVE GIFFORD

h
*Hodder
Children's
Books*

A division of Hachette Children's Books

© Copyright Hodder Children's Books 2007

Published in Great Britain in 2007 by Hodder Children's Books

Editor: Isabel Thurston
Design by Fiona Webb
Cover design: Hodder Children's Books

1

ISBN-10: 0 340 93126 4
ISBN-13: 978 0 340 93126 4

Printed by Bookmarque Ltd, Croydon, Surrey

The paper and board used in this paperback by Hodder Children's
Books are natural recyclable products made from wood grown in
sustainable forests. The manufacturing processes conform to the
environmental regulations of the
country of origin.

Hodder Children's Books
a division of Hachette Children's Books
338 Euston Road
London NW1 3BH

CONTENTS

INTRODUCTION

So you think you know all about William Shakespeare and his works? Reckon you can recall many of the playwright's amazing plays, poems and sonnets, the beautifully described characters and their actions and words? Contained in this book are over 1000 questions on Shakespeare's key works. Fifteen of Shakespeare's most popular plays each have their own dedicated quiz, and there are further quizzes on William Shakespeare's life, his other plays and the poems and sonnets. Enjoy Shakespeare's rich language, comic prose and lyrical poems as well as the twisting and turning plots as you tackle the questions. The answers are at the back of the book.

About the Author

Clive Gifford is an award-winning author of children's fiction and non-fiction, with titles as varied as *Kelly's Smelly Wellies* for young children to *Media and Communication* for teenagers. He is the author of all the *So You Think You Know* quiz books including titles on *The Lord of the Rings*, Terry Pratchett's *Discworld* and *Narnia*.

CURTAIN OPENING QUIZ

1. Was William Shakespeare born in Stretford, Stratford-upon-Avon or Streatham?

2. In collected editions of Shakespeare's plays, the plays are listed in four groups. One of these groups is called Tragedies – can you name any of the others?

3. In which play would you find these characters: Bottom, Quince, Puck and Titania?

4. In which play does a king shun one daughter and give his kingdom to the other two?

5. How many witches appear at the start of *Macbeth*?

6. From which play does the famous quote, 'To be, or not to be – that is the question?' come?

7. In which Italian city does the play *Julius Caesar* open?

8. What name, beginning with the letter S, is given to a type of short verse, of which Shakespeare wrote many?

9. Is *Hamlet*, *King Lear* or *Richard III* Shakespeare's longest play, with 4024 lines?

10. Which of the following is not one of Shakespeare's history plays: *King John*, *Richard II*, *King Lear* or *Edward III*?

11. Which play is called 'the Scottish play' by actors, who consider it unlucky to mention its name in a theatre?

12. Which of the following is not one of Shakespeare's tragedies: *Hamlet*, *Timon of Athens*, *The Merchant of Venice*, *Julius Caesar*?

13. Is *Titus Andronicus* set mainly in Ancient Greece, Ancient Rome, Ancient Carthage or Tudor England?

14. In which play does a moneylender insist on 'a pound of flesh': *The Merry Wives of Windsor*, *The Merchant of Venice* or *The Comedy of Errors*?

15. Is *The Phoenix and the Turtle* a play, a sonnet or a poem?

16. Which of the following is not one of Shakespeare's romance plays: *Love's Labour's Lost, The Winter's Tale, The Two Noble Kinsmen*?

17. Does Isabella, Juliet or Mistress Overdone cry for justice repeatedly at the city gates in *Measure For Measure*?

18. *Troilus and Cressida* is set during which major war of the Ancient World?

19. Sir Andrew Aguecheek appears in which Shakespeare comedy?

20. Which play tells the tale of a doomed romance between members of the warring Montague and Capulet families?

21. In *Titus Andronicus*, can you name either of the parts of Lavinia's body that are cut off when she is attacked?

22. In which play set in Ancient Roman times, does the wife of Brutus die by swallowing hot coal?

23. In which country is *Hamlet* largely set?

24. Which Shakespeare comedy features lovers getting mixed up in a forest, enchanted fairies and a craftsman whose head is turned into that of an ass?

25. Which of the following is not one of Shakespeare's tragedies: *Coriolanus, Cymbeline, Othello, Hamlet*?

26. In *Julius Caesar*, who gives the famous speech beginning, 'Friends, Romans, countrymen, lend me your ears …?

27. Does *Twelfth Night, Love's Labour's Lost* or *Much Ado About Nothing* feature a brother and sister who are twins?

28. Which play depicts the battle for the crown of Scotland and features characters including Fleance, Malcolm and King Duncan?

29. In which play would you find the female characters Bianca, Emilia and Desdemona?

30. What is the name of the friar the Duke disguises himself as, in *Measure For Measure*: Duncan, Petruchio or Ludowick?

31. Which of the following is not one of Shakespeare's comedies: *Troilus and Cressida, The Taming of the Shrew* or *The Tempest*?

32. Which comedy is the shortest of Shakespeare's plays, measuring 1786 lines in length?

33. 'He hath eaten me out of house and home,' is a quote from: *Henry IV Part II*, *Love's Labour's Lost* or *Julius Caesar*?

34. In *The Merry Wives of Windsor*, who is tricked by Ford and the wives and admits in Act 5 that, 'I do begin to perceive that I am made an ass'?

35. In *Troilus and Cressida*, who was a wife of Menelaus but now lives with Paris?

36. In *Julius Caesar*, does Brutus, Titinius or Cassius stab Caesar, lead an army to defeat against Mark Antony and order Strato to hold his sword so that he can fall on it and die?

37. Can you give the title of one of Shakespeare's tragedies that starts with the letter M?

38. Henry Bolingbroke becomes which English king: Henry IV, Henry V or Henry VI?

39. Can you recall the names of any of the three women who accompany the Princess of France when she visits Navarre in *Love's Labour's Lost*?

40. In *The Merry Wives of Windsor*, who marries Fenton: Anne Page, Mistress Ford or Mistress Quickly?

41. Which play features a fierce Roman warrior who switches sides but is eventually murdered by his greatest enemy: *The Tempest*, *Coriolanus* or *The Comedy of Errors*?

42. In *The Comedy of Errors*, what name, shared by the twins, begins with the letter D?

43. Which play features a Prince of Denmark and is considered by many people to be Shakespeare's greatest work?

44. Which member of her family kills Lavinia in *Titus Andronicus*?

45. In which Shakespeare romance does a man travel to Antioch, Tarsus, Pentapolis and Ephesus believing his wife and his daughter are dead, only to be reunited with them at the end?

46. In *The Comedy of Errors*, laws prevent trade between which two of the following towns: Ephesus, Rome, Syracuse, Naples?

47. 'The miserable have no other medicine but only hope' is a famous quotation from: *Macbeth, Measure for Measure* or *The Merry Wives of Windsor*?

48. In *The Two Noble Kinsmen*, is Hippolyta to marry Theseus, Arcite or Valerius?

49. Can you add the last two missing words to the famous line from *A Midsummer Night's Dream* which begins, 'The course of true love never did ___ ___'?

50. Who reveals to the duke, Valentine's plans to elope with Silvia in *The Two Gentlemen of Verona*?

SHAKESPEARE'S LIFE AND TIMES

1. What was the name of the famous theatre where most of Shakespeare's middle and later period plays were presented?

2. Was Shakespeare's father called John, Harry, Walter or Thomas?

3. In which century was Shakespeare born: 14th, 15th, 16th or 17th?

4. What was the name of Shakespeare's wife?

5. How old was Shakespeare's only son when he died?

6. Who were not permitted to act in plays during Elizabethan times: women, foreigners or poor people?

7. Was the name given to the first known published collection of Shakespeare plays, *The Workes, First Folio* or *The Dramatic Artes of William Shakespeare*?

8. In 1603, when Shakespeare was at the height of his powers, which king or queen died?

9. Did the Globe theatre burn down in 1613 during a performance of *King Lear, Othello, Henry VIII* or *The Comedy of Errors*?

10. In which city was the original Globe theatre constructed?

11. In Shakespeare's day, were poor theatregoers who stood in front of the stage known as stall-warts, groundlings or penny-pinchers?

12. How many of Shakespeare's history plays featured a king called Henry in their title?

13. Did Shakespeare die on St George's, St David's or St Patrick's Day, 1616?

14. In Shakespeare's time, any new play could only be performed after permission from: The Lord Chancellor, The Court of Jesters And Carousers or The Master of the Revels?

15. How many of William Shakespeare's eight brothers and sisters outlived him?

16. Who wrote Shakespeare's epitaph, the words that appear on his gravestone?

17. Was Shakespeare's First Folio published before or after his death?

18. Shakespeare's early long poems were dedicated to which patron: Sir Walter Raleigh, the Earl of Southampton, the Duke of Bedford or Queen Elizabeth I?

19. Did a reconstruction of the Globe theatre open near the original site in 1962, 1979, 1997 or 2003?

20. Was Mary Arden Shakespeare's mistress, his mother or the person who sponsored his early plays?

21. In front of which king was *The Tempest* first performed in 1611?

22. Which one of the following was not a rival theatre to the Globe set on the south bank of the River Thames: The Swan, The Rose, The Hope, The Comfort?

23. Although Shakespeare's father is believed to have worked as a wool trader and a moneylender, had he first trained as a hat maker, glove maker, cobbler or baker?

24. Could the original Globe theatre hold over 250, 600, 950 or 1500 people?

25. Which queen ruled England during the early years of Shakespeare's life?

26. Which of the following was not one of William Shakespeare's brothers: Gilbert, Thomas, Edmund or Richard?

27. Did the Globe theatre open in 1582, 1599, 1604 or 1613?

28. Some theatres closed and people left London in 1592 because of: a great fire, a war with France or an outbreak of plague?

29. Have over 25, over 35 or over 45 of Shakespeare's full-length plays survived to this day?

30. What was the last play that Shakespeare completed, believed to have been in 1614?

31. What was displayed at theatres during Shakespeare's time to show that a performance was under way?

32. Shakespeare joined the Lord Chamberlain's Men in the mid-1590s. Were they an honorary guard for Queen Elizabeth I, a theatre company or the society that ruled on which plays could be performed?

33. What is the name of the theatre company associated with Shakespeare, which got its current name in 1961 but whose history stretches back to the building of a theatre in Stratford in 1875?

34. Was Shakespeare buried in St Paul's Cathedral, Holy Trinity church, Stratford or Westminster Abbey?

35. The theatre company Shakespeare was associated with was renamed in 1603 following the crowning of King James I. What was its new name?

36. Was Shakespeare's first published long poem *Venus and Adonis*, *The Rape of Lucrece* or *A Lover's Complaint*?

37. Which play follows on from the three Henry VI plays to complete Shakespeare's first history play sequence?

38. Was Shakespeare's wife eight years younger, four years younger, four years older or eight years older than him?

39. Between 1604 and 1607, Shakespeare wrote three of his greatest plays, all tragedies. Can you name two of them?

40. The motto at the Globe theatre was, 'The whole world is a playhouse'. In which play did Shakespeare modify this motto to write the line, 'All the world's a stage ...'?

41. Can the words, 'Blest be the man that spares these stones, /And curst be he that moves my bones' be found in Shakespeare's last play, in his will, on his gravestone or inscribed on his house in Stratford?

42. What colour flag was used to signify a history play being performed at the Globe theatre?

43. The tiring room at theatres in Shakespeare's day was: where the box office money was counted, where actors changed costume or where audience members who stole or were drunk were held until soldiers came?

44. Which ruler of England was fascinated by witchcraft, a fact that is believed to have prompted Shakespeare to include witches in *Macbeth*?

45. What was the flower-based name of the London theatre believed to have staged Shakespeare's first plays?

46. Shakespeare and his wife had twins. Can you recall either of their names?

47. England's King James I was supposed to be a descendant of which character from the play, *Macbeth*?

48. What three-letter word, beginning with the letter P, was given to the open air area in front of the stage of theatres in Shakespeare's day where people would pay the least to stand and watch?

49. Did Shakespeare write 37, 86 or 154 sonnets?

50. In 1596, Shakespeare bought a grand house in Stratford for his family. Do you know what it was called?

KING LEAR

1. How many daughters does King Lear have?

2. Who is Lear's eldest daughter?

3. Who is Lear's youngest daughter?

4. After giving a portion of his kingdom to his daughters which one of them does King Lear visit first?

5. Which nobleman has his eyes plucked out by Cornwall and Regan?

6. Who plots to remove Edgar from his inheritance by spreading false rumours of Edgar's plans to murder his father?

7. Which of his daughters prompts Lear to fly into a rage in Act 1, and eventually to disown her?

8. Who claims her only joy in life is loving her father?

9. Does Edgar, Lear or Oswald lead the blinded Earl of Gloucester through the countryside?

10. Which character appears to have signed the letter which contains the sentence, 'If our father would sleep till I wak'd him, you should enjoy half his revenue for ever …'?

11. Who takes off his own clothing to help keep Poor Tom warm during the storm?

12. Who insists that Lear reduces the number of followers accompanying him to her house by half from 100 to 50?

13. When Edgar and Edmund fight in single combat in Act 5, who wins?

14. Which character, apart from Kent, leaves Goneril's castle with Lear after he departs in a rage?

15. Can you name either of the noblemen attending King Lear's court who were hoping to marry Cordelia?

16. During the storm when Lear, the Fool and Kent in disguise seek shelter, who do they find in the hovel?

17. In which act of the play are Cordelia and Lear reunited, with Lear saying, 'If you have poison for me, I will drink it'?

18. How many days is the Earl of Kent given to leave King Lear's kingdom?

19. Who calls Goneril and Regan 'unnatural hags' in Act 2?

20. What is the name of the eldest son of the Earl of Gloucester?

21. Does Regan insist on Lear cutting the number of his followers when he stays with her to 75, 50, 25 or 10?

22. In Act 3, which country may declare war: France, Spain or Bohemia?

23. Does Albany, Kent or Gloucester appeal to Lear saying, 'My lord, I am guiltless, as I am ignorant/Of what hath moved you …'?

24. Who did King Lear strike for being rude about the Fool?

25. Who is forced to sleep in the stocks for the night by Regan and Cornwall?

26. Which of Lear's daughters tells him, 'Unhappy that I am, I cannot heave/ My heart into my mouth. I love your majesty /According to my bond; no more nor less'?

27. In Act 1, does Kent say he is 28, 38, 48 or 58 when he says 'I have years on my back'?

28. What name does Edgar go under when he disguises himself as a penniless beggar?

29. Which of King Lear's daughters says to him, 'Sir, I love you more than word can wield the matter;/Dearer than eyesight, space and liberty'?

30. Who kills Oswald as he is carrying a message from Goneril to Edmund?

31. The Duke of Albany is married to which of Lear's daughters?

32. Who says these words after being punished and injured: 'As flies to wanton boys are we to the gods/They kill us for their sport'?

33. Where does Gloucester ask to be taken so that he can commit suicide?

34. Which of Cordelia's suitors withdraws interest on learning that she will not inherit a portion of King Lear's kingdom?

35. Which nobleman disguises himself as a poor man called Caius to serve at King Lear's court?

36. Who says of King Lear, 'By day and night he wrongs me. Every hour/He flashes into one gross crime or other'?

37. Which two women start to fight for the attentions of Edmund?

38. When he plucks out Gloucester's second eye, does Cornwall say, 'Upon these eyes of thine I'll set my foot', 'Lest it see more, prevent it./ Out, vile jelly!' or 'Blind thou art to thy sins'?

39. Who is the illegitimate son of the Earl of Gloucester: Edgar, Edmund, Edward or Erasmus?

40. Can you finish the first sentence of the speech that Lear delivers at the start of Act 2, Scene 2 which begins with 'Blow, winds, and …'?

41. Who carries Cordelia's body to the others in the final scene and dies of grief shortly afterwards?

42. Who is King Lear's middle daughter, Regan, married to?

43. Who says, 'Why have my sisters husbands, if they say/They love you all?'?

44. Is King Lear over 50, over 60, over 70 or over 80?

45. Can you complete the quote from Act 1, 'How sharper than a serpent's tooth ...'?

46. Is Goneril's steward called Oswald, Edgar or Curan?

47. Who poisons her sister then kills herself?

48. Which nobleman loyal to King Lear does he banish in Act 1?

49. In the Fool's speech in Act 1, what line follows, 'Have more than thou showest ...'?

50. Who is the Fool speaking to when he says the rhyme above: Goneril, King Lear, Cordelia or Regan?

HENRY V

1. What is the name of the character, beginning with the letter C, whose speeches open each act of the play?

2. What is the name of the great battle that occurs in the play, beginning with the letter A?

3. By what other name beginning with the letter H is King Henry V also known?

4. Warwick says that the French army numbers 'threescore thousand'. How many soldiers is that?

5. Was Nim, Pistol or Bardolph to be executed in Act 3 for stealing?

6. Was Captain MacMorris, Gower or Fluellen in charge of digging the tunnels under the walls of Harfleur?

7. What is the name of the French princess King Henry marries?

8. In which Act does King Henry order the execution of the three noblemen who were traitors?

9. Who is the ruler of France at the beginning of the play?

10. From what town in southern England does Henry plan to set sail for France?

11. Which Lord is bribed to kill Henry in the play: Scrope, Gower or Montjoy?

12. Is the Duke of Clarence, Cornwall or Caithness the brother of King Henry V?

13. After the battle at Agincourt, the English forces have lost just 25 men and how many lords?

14. Who does the Archbishop of Canterbury say had, 'His hours filled up with riots, banquets, sports,/And never noted in him any study'?

15. Who urges, 'God, the best maker of all marriages,/Combine your hearts in one, your realms in one'?

16. Which Duke's forces are left to guard Harfleur as King Henry presses on towards Calais?

17. The Governor of which town surrenders to Henry V saying, 'We yield our town and lives to thy soft mercy'?

18. The Dauphin is the heir to the throne of which country?

19. In Act 1, with which other religious figure does the Archbishop of Canterbury discuss the transformation of Henry from wild young prince to mature king?

20. Is Captain Jamy English, Scottish or Welsh?

21. Which of King Henry's cousins is killed at Agincourt?

22. Which knight does the hostess say has gone to 'Arthur's bosom' when he dies?

23. Was the traitor, Sir Thomas Grey, from Cornwall, Warwickshire or Northumberland?

24. Who utters the famous speech which begins, 'Once more unto the breach, dear friends, once more …'?

25. As this speech is made, are the English troops outside Harfleur, Calais or Agincourt?

26. When King Henry V borrows Sir Thomas Erpingham's cloak and pretends to be an ordinary soldier, who is the first soldier he speaks to, saying his name, 'sorts well with your fierceness'?

27. Which religious figure is the first character to speak in Act 1 of the play?

28. What is the name of the officer who beats Nim to get him back to battle?

29. Is the Duke of Exeter, Bedford or York, King Henry V's brother?

30. Does Bardolph, Nell Quickly or Doll Tearsheet draw a sword to stop Pistol and Nim from fighting, saying, 'He that strikes the first stroke, I'll run him up to the hilts'?

31. What language is Princess Katherine secretly learning in the French court?

32. Which Duke opens the barrel from the French ambassador and tells Henry what is contained inside?

33. Can you complete the final line of the speech beginning, 'Cry, "God for Harry ..."' which Henry makes to his forces?

34. Is Captain MacMorris from Scotland, Ireland or Wales?

35. At what tavern is Nell Quickly the innkeeper's wife?

36. What is the name of Princess Katherine's attendant who helps her learn a foreign language?

37. Which friend of Nim, Pistol and Bardolph dies in Act 2?

38. The Boy says that which two characters, '... are sworn brothers of filching, and in Calais they stole a fire shovel'?

39. What does King Henry instruct Exeter to fill the glove with to give to the soldier, Williams?

40. What vegetable does Pistol insult Fluellen for carrying as a symbol of his country, resulting in Pistol receiving a beating?

41. When King Charles is offering his daughter to King Henry what line follows: 'In their sweet bosoms, that never war advance ...'?

42. Who: learns that his wife has died; is forced to eat a leek and decides to return to England to become a thief?

43. What is the name of the herald that King Charles VI sends to King Henry to ask the English forces to withdraw?

44. Is King Henry V in Southampton, London, Calais or Paris when he unmasks the three noblemen as traitors plotting to kill him?

45. At the start of Act 4, do the French forces outnumber the English ones by two to one, three to one, four to one or five to one?

46. Which soldier did Nell Quickly marry instead of Nim?

47. What do the disguised King Henry and the soldier, Michael Williams exchange, signalling their intent to possibly duel in the future?

48. Which knight was part of the group bribed to kill King Henry V?

49. What is contained in the barrel given to Henry by a French ambassador in Act 1?

50. Does King Charles VI of France, the Duke of Exeter or King Henry V threaten a town with the image of 'your naked infants spitted upon pikes' unless they surrender?

THE TAMING OF THE SHREW

1. Who tames Katharina's (Kate's) wild temper in the play?

2. What is the name of Kate's younger sister?

3. On what day of the week does Petruchio arrange to marry Kate?

4. Can you name either of Lucentio's servants?

5. Who throws a banquet to celebrate his own and the other marriages at the end of the play?

6. Which brash character declares that, 'I come to wive it wealthily in Padua'?

7. Does Sly say he is a cardmaker, tailor, tinker or baker by education?

8. How many suitors does Bianca have in the play?

9. Do the Lord and his staff say Sly has been asleep for five, ten or fifteen years?

10. In Act 4, who arrives at Petruchio's house to see his 'taming school'?

11. In the induction at the start, does the Lord, Christopher Sly, Gremio or Bartholomew say to the hostess that, 'I will not budge an inch'?

12. What musical instrument does Kate smash over the head of her music tutor, Cambio?

13. Baptista Minola is a gentleman from Padua, Venice, Messina or Bordeaux?

14. Who strikes the priest, swears at the altar and throws food on his own wedding day?

15. Does Hortensio disguise himself as Bianca's Latin, music or French tutor?

16. Which of Bianca's suitors is the oldest: Gremio, Hortensio or Lucentio?

17. Does Tranio, disguised as Lucentio, offer three times, five times or ten times whatever Gremio offers in order to marry Bianca?

18. What name does Lucentio give when disguised as a tutor: Licio, Tranio, Cambio or Grumio?

19. To which city does Petruchio announce that he is off to buy wedding clothes?

20. When the three newly-married men devise a test to see which of their wives is the most obedient, is the winner Kate, the widow or Bianca?

21. Who gives Bianca a Latin passage to translate which actually reveals his love for her?

22. Who has to get married first before Bianca is allowed to marry?

23. Who sternly tells Kate over a disagreement about time, 'It shall be what o'clock I say it is'?

24. Who says of Bianca to Baptista, 'She is your treasure, she must have a husband. I must dance barefoot on her wedding day'?

25. 'That wench is stark mad' is the conclusion drawn by Tranio, Gremio or Lucentio after watching Kate for only a few moments?

26. Who gives up trying to woo Bianca and instead marries a widow?

27. As what sort of tutor does Lucentio disguise himself as so as to be close to Bianca?

28. Can you recall Kate's response to Petruchio saying, 'Come, come, you wasp, i'faith you are too angry'?

29. Near the end of Act 2, about which of Bianca's suitors' offers of wealth does Baptista say, 'I must confess your offer is the best'?

30. Which character in the play cries, 'O, I am undone, I am undone! While I play the good husband at home, my son and my servant spend all at the university.'?

31. Petruchio refuses to continue their journey until Kate admits that the sun is what other object?

32. Is Petruchio's old friend Hortensio, Lucentio or Gremio?

33. At the start of the play, the Lord who plays a trick on Christopher Sly has just returned from doing what?

34. Who strikes Bianca shortly after asking her whether she loves Gremio or Hortensio?

35. Whose father is alarmed to find a servant impersonating his son in Padua?

36. At the start of Act 4, as part of his plan to 'curb her mad and headstrong humour', does Petruchio not let Kate eat, see her family or wear any clothes?

37. Who does Bianca finally marry?

38. What does Tranio say about Kate straight after Gremio says of Petruchio, 'Why he's a devil, a devil, a very fiend'?

39. Can you change one letter of Gremio to come up with the name of Petruchio's servant?

40. Who arrives at his own wedding in outrageous clothing but when the father of the bride protests, answers, 'To me she's married, not unto my clothes'?

41. Who tells Kate off, saying, 'For shame, thou hilding of a devilish spirit'?

42. Who surprises others in Act 5 by making a speech which includes the lines, 'Thy husband is thy lord, thy life, thy keeper,/Thy head, thy sovereign, one that cares for thee'?

43. The servant, Curtis, remarks that he thinks which character is more like a shrew than Kate?

44. Can you complete the line, 'Strive mightily ...' uttered by Tranio disguised as Lucentio when he suggests that the three suitors for Bianca compete but try to get along?

45. Which character begins a speech in the last scene of the play that starts, 'Fie, fie! unknit that threat'ning, unkind brow,/And dart not scornful glances from those eyes'?

46. Who wakes up from being drunk at the start of the play to be tricked into believing he is a lord?

47. Does Petruchio, Grumio or Lucentio say to Hortensio, 'Katherine the curst!/A title for a maid, of all titles the worst'?

48. The schoolmaster dressed up as Lucentio's father, tries to get which character arrested, saying, 'Lay hands on the villain'?

49. Who makes an entrance at the start of Act 2 with bound hands?

50. The Lord's servant Bartholomew helps trick Sly by pretending to be Sly's: brother, servant, son or wife?

THE TEMPEST

1. What is a tempest: a magician, a storm or the name of an island?

2. What is the name of the magician who was once Duke of Milan?

3. Is Caliban a nobleman, a sailor, a ghost or a slave?

4. Is Iris a spirit that appears in the masque, Alonso's serving girl or Prospero's wife?

5. What is the name of Prospero's daughter?

6. Who says, 'By accident most strange, bountiful Fortune,/Now my dear lady, hath mine enemies/Brought to this shore'?

7. Who is called, 'A devil, a born devil, on whose nature/Nurture can never stick'?

8. Who hides and watches Miranda and Ferdinand declare their love for each other in Act 3?

9. According to Sebastian, Alonso, depressed at losing his son, 'receives comfort like ...' what?

10. Who says to Prospero, 'You taught me language; and my profit on't/Is, I know how to curse'?

11. Does Miranda say that Prospero, Caliban or Ferdinand is 'the third man that e'er I saw'?

12. Who does Caliban offer to serve instead of Prospero?

13. Does Antonio, Gonzalo or Ferdinand say of the island, 'Here is everything advantageous to life'?

14. What item of Prospero's does Caliban say must be possessed first as without them he is powerless?

15. Can you name two of the three characters who stagger drunkenly around the island?

16. Does Caliban, Prospero or Gonzalo say, 'The strongest oaths are straw,/To th' fire i' th' blood'?

17. Fill in the missing word of the line uttered by Prospero whilst watching the masque, 'I had forgot that foul conspiracy/Of the beast _____ and his confederates/Against my life;'?

18. Who says, 'O, I have suffered/With those that I saw suffer!' at the sight of the shipwreck?

19. Who makes an aside about Ferdinand and Miranda that, 'They are both in each other's powers'?

20. About whom is said, 'That's a brave god, and bears celestial liquor/I will kneel to him …'?

21. Can you recall the second line of Prospero's epilogue, the first line being, 'Now my charms are all o'erthrown'?

22. To whom does Prospero say, 'I have given you a third of mine own life'?

23. Does Prospero force Ferdinand to dig a new boat harbour, carry wood, herd goats or wash his feet?

24. Is the ship carrying Alonso that gets wrecked in the storm returning from a wedding in Rome, Madrid, Tunis or Istanbul?

25. Does Prospero release spirits in the form of hounds, giant fish or lions to chase Stefano and the others in Act 4?

26. About whom does Alonso ask, 'Is she the goddess that hath severed us,/And brought us thus together'?

27. Who persuades Sebastian to attempt to kill Alonso and Gonzalo so that Sebastian can become king?

28. Who shows faith in the boatswain when their ship is hit by a storm saying, 'I have great comfort from this fellow. Methinks he hath no drowning mark upon him;'?

29. When Ariel claps his wings, does Ferdinand, a banquet, Prospero or a ship disappear in front of Sebastian, Alonso and Antonio's eyes?

30. Is Prospero's brother Alonso, Sebastian or Antonio?

31. Who plays music that sends all but Sebastian and Antonio to sleep?

32. Who urges Alonso to cheer up shortly after being shipwrecked, saying, 'You have cause,/So have we all, of joy; for our escape/Is much beyond our loss.'?

33. Have Prospero and Miranda been on the island for two, six, eight or twelve years?

34. What will Prospero be doing in the afternoon at the time that Caliban suggests to Stefano that they murder him?

35. Who had succeeded Prospero as the Duke of Milan?

36. Was Caliban's mother, Sycorax, a queen, a witch or a poor washerwoman?

37. Who says, 'Monster, I will kill this man' meaning Prospero, and adds, 'His daughter and I will be king and queen – save our graces!'?

38. Is Trinculo, Gonzalo or Stefano the court jester to the King of Naples?

39. Who marries Miranda?

40. What game are Miranda and Ferdinand playing when Alonso is reunited with his son?

41. According to Sebastian, is the heir to the throne of Naples: Miranda, Claribel or Gonzalo?

42. What shape does Prospero draw on the ground in Act 5 which traps Alonso and the others inside it?

43. Who renounces magic in return for regaining his title back in Italy?

44. To whom does Prospero speak when he says, 'Let them be hunted soundly. At this hour/ Lies at my mercy all mine enemies. /Shortly shall my labours end, and thou/Shalt have the air at freedom;'?

45. Which member of Antonio's court had many years earlier helped Prospero flee with his books?

46. Which character had Caliban once tried to rape?

47. What is the name of Prospero's spirit, which he has summoned to create a storm that causes the shipwreck?

48. Which character does Prospero take prisoner by magic in Act 1?

49. Who says that the island is full of noises and, 'Sometimes a thousand twangling instruments/ Will hum about mine ears;'?

50. When Gonzalo awakes to find Sebastian and Antonio with their swords drawn, what creature does Sebastian say they were trying to fend off?

ANTONY AND CLEOPATRA

1. At the very start of the play is Mark Antony (Antony) in Rome, Messina or Egypt?

2. How many co-rulers of Rome are there at the start of the play?

3. Who does Antony marry during the play but leave for Cleopatra?

4. Why does Sextus Pompey want revenge on Rome: because he was banished as a child, to avenge the death of his father or to recover his imprisoned wife?

5. Which character kills himself rather than kill Antony?

6. Does Charmian, Eros or the Soothsayer in Act 1 say to Cleopatra, 'In time we hate that which we often fear'?

7. Who, whilst plotting his rise to power says, 'I shall do well. The people love me, and the sea is mine'?

8.   What title, beginning with the letter T, is given to the co-rulers of Rome?

9.   Antony names Cleopatra 'absolute Queen' of: Parthia, Syria, the Roman Empire or Turkey?

10. What fruit is found in the basket containing the deadly snakes that kill Cleopatra?

11. Who strikes a messenger down on hearing the news that Antony has married Octavia?

12. Which one of the following is not a friend or follower of Antony: Eros, Alexas, Silius or Scarus?

13. Who says to Antony, 'You take from me a great part of myself;/ Use me well in't. Sister, prove such a wife/As my thoughts make thee …'?

14. Which of the Triumvir has a name beginning with the letter L?

15. Which rival of Antony's for power is the great-nephew of Julius Caesar?

16. Who says, 'This foul Egyptian hath betrayed me … Like a right gipsy hath at fast and loose/Beguil'd me to the very heart of loss'?

17. Can you recall the names of either of Cleopatra's attendants, who the soothsayer states will outlive the queen?

18. On which two parts of her body does Cleopatra place the deadly snakes before dying: her arm, leg, chest, neck, back or head?

19. Who says of Antony and Cleopatra's grave that, 'No grave upon the earth shall clip in it/A pair so famous …'?

20. Which one of the following is not a friend or follower of Octavius Caesar: Scarus, Agrippa or Gallus?

21. How does Mark Antony die?

22. Does a clown, Dolabella or Charmian bring Cleopatra the basket containing the deadly snakes that kill her?

23. In which city is Antony when he learns that Caesar has denounced him in the senate in Rome?

24. Whose first line in the play is, 'If it be love indeed, tell me how much?'?

25. Can you complete Enobarbus's line as he makes a speech praising Cleopatra: 'Age cannot wither her ...'?

26. What precious piece of jewellery does Antony send Cleopatra in Act 1?

27. Who laments that his leader has become, 'a strumpet's fool' at the very start of the play?

28. What was the soothsayer's answer to Antony's question, 'Whose fortunes shall rise higher: Caesar's or mine?'?

29. Does Lepidus, Agrippa or Proculeius suggest that Antony should marry Octavia?

30. Who says, 'I am dying, Egypt, dying; only/ I here importune death awhile until/Of many thousand kisses the poor last/I lay upon thy lips'?

31. Is Selecus Cleopatra's chief of guards, her treasurer, a court jester or an assassin?

32. Does Antony go himself, send Ventidius or send Philo and Demetrius to lead the fight against the Parthian forces?

33. Which of the play's acts has a total of sixteen different scenes?

34. Who vows to send Antony, 'a several greeting' every day whilst he is away from Egypt?

35. When a servant says, 'Lepidus is high coloured' at the party on Pompey's galley do they mean he is: drunk, cheerful or angry and argumentative?

36. How many ships does Cleopatra offer Antony to fight Caesar's forces at sea: 10, 30, 60 or 100?

37. Which loyal servant of Cleopatra's also dies of a snake bite?

38. Which one of the following is not in league with Sextus Pompey: Menas, Proculeius, Varrius or Menecrates?

39. Who says, 'I am alone the villain of the earth' and later, when dying, 'But let the world rank me in register/A master-leaver and a fugitive!'?

40. Who, worried about Antony returning to Rome, says, 'Now I see, I see/In Fulvia's death how mine receiv'd shall be'?

41. Does Menas, Pompey or Menecrates suggest murdering Antony, Octavius and Lepidus when they board Pompey's galley?

42. Whose apparent death spurs Antony on to take his own life?

43. An envoy in Act 1 brings news that Parthian forces have invaded which country?

44. Who sends a message to ask Cleopatra to leave Antony?

45. Does Cleopatra, Antony or Lepidus say in Act 1, 'Let Rome in Tiber melt, and the wide arch/Of the rang'd empire fall!'?

46. In Act 3 Scene 3, who is referred to as, 'Dull of tongue and dwarfish': Caesar, Lepidus, Enobarbus or Octavia?

47. When Antony says, 'The April's in her eyes. It is love's spring,' is he saying Octavia is laughing, asleep or crying?

48. At the start of the play to whom is Antony married?

49. Who insists on leaving Pompey's galley as the party gets wilder saying, 'Our graver business/Frowns at this levity'?

50. Does Iras die of a snake bite, a sword or of sorrow that Cleopatra is dying?

HAMLET

1. What title does Hamlet have at the start of the play?

2. How does Ophelia die: by poison, a sword or drowning?

3. Complete the famous line, 'To be, or not to be ...'?

4. What is the name of the courtier, beginning with the letter O, who arranges the duel between Hamlet and Laertes?

5. Who does Hamlet ask to keep an eye on Claudius for signs of guilt as the play is performed?

6. Fortinbras is a prince from which country?

7. Who sends Reynaldo abroad to spy on Laertes?

8. What is the name of the castle in Denmark at which the play begins?

9. Can you name any one of the three soldiers at the opening of the play?

10. At which university, beginning with the letter W, had Hamlet been a student?

11. Is Laertes, Horatio or Rosencrantz the son of Polonius?

12. What role in King Hamlet's court was once played by Yorick?

13. Can you complete the rest of the line that follows, 'Whether 'tis nobler in the mind to suffer …' in Act 3, spoken by Hamlet?

14. At the end of Act 2 when Hamlet plots his play revealing Claudius's guilt in killing his father, how does this line continue: 'The play's the thing …'?

15. Whose sword is covered in poison so that it will kill Hamlet if it strikes him?

16. When King Claudius asks Hamlet the name of his play, what does Hamlet reply?

17. Who says to Hamlet, 'I pray thee stay with us, not go to Wittenberg': Gertrude, Ophelia or Horatio?

18. Who plans for Hamlet to be killed on arriving in England?

19. Does Hamlet call Ophelia, Gildenstern or Rosencrantz, 'a sponge' that soaks up the 'King's countenance, his rewards, his authorities'?

20. Does to 'shuffle off this mortal coil' mean to get married, to plot revenge, to die or to sleep?

21. In the play designed by Hamlet to catch out Claudius, does the murderer pour poison into the king's mouth, his ear or his clothing?

22. In Act 5, who declares, 'I am justly kill'd with mine own treachery'?

23. Just before his play begins, Hamlet asks Polonius about his acting career. Which character, the name of another Shakespeare play, does Polonius say he once played?

24. Who orders four captains to bear Hamlet's dead body and give him a military funeral?

25. Complete the missing three words from the lines Hamlet utters on hearing of Ophelia's death: 'I lov'd Ophelia: _____ _____ _____ /Could not, with all their quantity of love,/ Make up my sum'?

26. Who does Hamlet force to drink poison, calling him, 'thou incestuous, murd'rous damned Dane'?

27. From which country does Laertes return to avenge the deaths of his father and sister?

28. The ghost that Hamlet sees and talks with is of which member of his family?

29. In the duel between Laertes and Hamlet, who draws the first blood?

30. Who is Polonius speaking to when he says, 'This above all: to thine own self be true'?

31. What is the name of Hamlet's mother, who remarries straight after his father's death?

32. Who says, 'When sorrows come, they come not single spies, but in battalions'?

33. Which grieving character is the first to leap into Ophelia's grave?

34. Who says of Hamlet, 'How dangerous it is that this man goes loose!'?

35. Can you complete the following line from Act 1 uttered by Marcellus, 'Something is rotten in …'?

36. Can you name either of the characters, old friends of Hamlet, who are hired by Claudius to spy on him?

37. Whose skull does Hamlet hold and recall as, '... a fellow of infinite jest, of most excellent fancy; he hath borne me on his back a thousand times.'?

38. At the start of Act 5, two clowns are digging whose grave?

39. Who is Ophelia's father: Claudius, Polonius, Laertes or Fortinbras?

40. To which country does Claudius intend to send Hamlet because he views him as a dangerous threat?

41. Who murders his own brother to become King of Denmark?

42. Who says of Hamlet that, 'He hath, my lord, of late made many tenders/Of his affection to me.'?

43. Who says of Queen Gertrude that she will 'prey on garbage'?

44. What line does Hamlet speak after saying to Ophelia, 'Get thee to a nunnery'?

45. Who will be the object of Hamlet's harsh words when he says, 'I will speak daggers to her, but use none'?

46. Who is the first to die from the poison in the goblet handed out by King Claudius?

47. As he dies, who does Hamlet say that he wants to rule Denmark: Horatio, Ophelia, Fortinbras or Reynaldo?

48. Whose ghost do Horatio and the soldiers see on the battlements of the castle in the first scene of the play?

49. Which character, before talking about Hamlet's madness, says, 'Since brevity is the soul of wit'?

50. Does Laertes, Gertrude or Claudius ask Hamlet to 'exchange forgiveness' before dying?

RICHARD III

1. Can you complete the line which begins, 'A horse! A horse! ...'?

2. How is the Duke of Clarence related to Richard, Duke of Gloucester?

3. How many murderers enter the Tower of London to kill the Duke of Clarence?

4. Is Cardinal Bourchier Archbishop of Westminster, Canterbury or York?

5. What is the name of the castle to which Lord Rivers and Lord Gray are sent as prisoners?

6. Is Henry VII, Richard II or Edward IV the king at the start of the play?

7. Which part of Richard Gloucester's body has been withered since birth: his arm, his foot, his leg or his hand?

8. Who murders the princes in the tower?

9. Is Brakenbury, Catesby, Tyrrel or Hastings the lieutenant in charge of the Tower of London?

10. To which prince was Lady Anne previously married?

11. Who calls Richard Gloucester a 'foul devil' yet later marries him?

12. Who says, 'So, now prosperity begins to mellow/And drop into the rotten mouth of death': Queen Margaret, Buckingham, Lord Stanley or Lady Anne?

13. What are the names of the two young princes imprisoned by Richard Gloucester?

14. Who does Richard Gloucester hand his sword to, offering her the chance to kill him?

15. Who kills King Richard III?

16. Does Tyrrel, Catesby, or Buckingham go to see Lord Hastings to determine whether he will support Richard Gloucester becoming king?

17. To which castle do a group of citizens organized by Buckingham go to ask Richard to become king?

18. After his father, King Edward IV's death, which prince becomes the heir to the throne?

19. Was John Morton the Bishop of Canterbury, Ely, Winchester or Norfolk?

20. What is the name of Richard III's wife, whom he has killed shortly after being crowned king?

21. Which former queen despises Richard and calls him, 'a poisonous hunch back'd toad' and a 'bottled spider'?

22. Can you complete the line which begins, 'So wise so young, they say …'?

23. Who says, 'Since I cannot prove a lover/ To entertain these fair well-spoken days,/ I am determined to prove a villain/And hate the idle pleasures of these days.'?

24. Who mistakenly thinks of Richard Gloucester as someone whose feelings are easy to read, saying, '… there's never a man in Christendom/Can lesser hide his love or hate than he,/For by his face straight shall you know his heart'?

25. In which country does Henry Tudor, Earl of Richmond, assemble his forces?

26. At what battlefield is King Richard III killed?

27. To whom does the ghost of Prince Edward say, 'Let me sit heavy on thy soul tomorrow'?

28. Is Sir Richard Ratcliffe a supporter or enemy of the new king, Richard III?

29. What is the first name of the lady the newly-crowned Richard III wants to marry?

30. Does Catesby, Hastings or Buckingham say, ' 'Tis a vile thing to die, my gracious lord,/ When men are unprepar'd and look not for it.'?

31. Which duke, his own brother, does Richard Gloucester manage to get the King to arrest and imprison in the Tower of London?

32. In Act 1, Richard Gloucester says that the world is grown so bad that what type of bird dares not perch?

33. Was Thomas Rotherham an archbishop, a duke, a hired murderer or a scribe?

34. Of whose death did a murderer say, 'A bloody deed, and desperately dispatch'd/ How fain, like Pilate, would I wash my hands/Of this most grievous, guilty murder!'?

35. In which tower are the young princes imprisoned?

36. Whose son is Edward Plantagenet?

37. Is Lord Stanley the Earl of Derby, Somerset, Norfolk or Lancaster?

38. In Act 3, Stanley tells Hastings of a nightmare he suffered, in which what creature attacked and killed him?

39. King Richard III takes which lord's son hostage in Act 4?

40. Was Sir James Blunt one of Richard's or one of Henry Tudor's followers?

41. Richard III says, 'Conscience is but a word that ...' who uses?

42. Can you recall the line that follows this: 'Now is the winter of our discontent ...'?

43. Who says to Richard Gloucester, 'Out of my sight! Thou dost infect mine eyes'?

44. Is England ruled by one, two, three or four different kings in total in the play?

45. Which king insists Buckingham and others should stop their feud and, 'swear your love'?

46. Was Queen Anne, Queen Mary or Queen Elizabeth the wife of King Edward IV?

47. Who is Richard Gloucester's mother: Queen Elizabeth, Queen Margaret or the Duchess of York?

48. In Act 2, does a cardinal give Queen Elizabeth, Lady Anne or the Duchess of York the Great Seal of England?

49. To which house does Richard Gloucester belong: Lancaster, York or Hampshire?

50. Is James Tyrrel, Robert Brakenbury or Thomas Rotherham the Archbishop of York?

ROMEO AND JULIET

1. What is the surname of Romeo's father?

2. Is *Romeo and Juliet* largely set in Venice, Paris, Verona or Pisa?

3. Who actually dies first: Romeo or Juliet?

4. In Act 3, who does Romeo kill in a fight, forcing him to flee?

5. What day of the week is set by Capulet and Paris for Paris's wedding to Juliet?

6. Does Peter, Abraham or Samson tell Romeo the guest list for the Capulets' feast?

7. Who gives Juliet a powerful potion to make it appear that she is dead?

8. Can you recall Romeo's last line before he dies, 'Thy drugs are quick. Thus …'?

9. Does Juliet, Capulet, Romeo or Paris say, 'My only love sprung from my only hate!/ Too early seen unknown, and known too late!'

10. In which Act does Romeo first see Juliet?

11. Which character, beginning with the letter B, brings Romeo news of the death of Juliet?

12. Who says, 'My ears have yet not drunk a hundred words/Of thy tongue's uttering, yet I know the sound'?

13. Where does Romeo head to in exile after the death of Tybalt?

14. Can you recall the famous line that Romeo utters immediately before, 'It is the east, and Juliet is the sun!'?

15. Who says, 'What's here? A cup clos'd in my true love's hand'?

16. Whose dead body does Romeo spy near to Juliet's in the tomb?

17. Are the lines: 'For never was a story of more woe, than this of Juliet and her Romeo', spoken at the very beginning of the play, the start of Act 4 or at the very end of the play?

18. What is the name of the nobleman friend of the Prince of Verona who expects to marry Juliet?

19. Who exiles Romeo for the killing of Tybalt?

20. What line does Juliet speak immediately after, 'O, Romeo, Romeo! wherefore art thou Romeo'?

21. 'Death is my son-in-law, Death is my heir,' are the sad words of which father who has lost a child?

22. Who wounds Mercutio, ultimately causing his death?

23. Who is Romeo in love with at the very beginning of the play?

24. Who tells the Prince of Verona that his wife has died of grief due to Romeo leaving Verona?

25. Who sets up a ladder made of cloth so that Romeo can climb to reach Juliet's room on their wedding night?

26. Does Benvolio, Montague or Mercutio advise Romeo, 'If love be rough with you, be rough with love'?

27. How old is Juliet in the play: thirteen, fifteen, seventeen or nineteen?

28. What is the name of the friar charged with the task of delivering the letter about Juliet's faked death to Romeo?

29. Who says, 'Sin from my lips? O trespass sweetly urg'd! Give me my sin again'?

30. Can you name either of the Capulet family servants, with biblical names, who at the start of the play engage in a brawl with servants from the Montague family?

31. Is Benvolio a member of the Montagues or the Capulets?

32. Who secretly marries Romeo and Juliet?

33. Who disturbs Romeo and Juliet the first time they kiss, saying that Juliet's mother wishes to see her?

34. Who spots Romeo at the Capulets' feast and orders a servant to bring his rapier?

35. Who cries to her husband, 'A crutch, a crutch – why call you for a sword'?

36. At the Capulets' feast in Act 1, Mercutio gives a speech about a fairy queen who brings dreams to sleepers. What was the fairy queen's name?

37. Who does Romeo kill just before entering Juliet's tomb?

38. Capulet asks Paris to wait for how many years before marrying his daughter?

39. Can you recall who speaks the very last lines of the play?

40. What relation to Romeo is Benvolio: uncle, brother, cousin or father?

41. Does Juliet die by poisoning, stabbing herself or throwing herself off a balcony?

42. Whose dying words include, 'A plague a both your houses! They have made worms' meat of me'?

43. An apothecary sells which character a deadly poison?

44. Who grieves for the death of Tybalt, saying, 'O Tybalt, Tybalt, the best friend I had!': Juliet, Juliet's nurse, Paris or Capulet?

45. Who, on learning the facts surrounding Romeo and Juliet's deaths, turns to Capulet and Montague and says, 'See what a scourge is laid upon your hate …'?

46. Who wears a mask just like Romeo's as he accompanies him to the Capulets' feast?

47. Who speaks to Juliet about Tybalt's death saying, 'Will you speak well of him that killed your cousin?'?

48. Who advises Romeo to calm his passion, saying, 'These violent delights have violent ends,/And in their triumph die; like fire and powder,/Which, as they kiss, consume.'?

49. After leaving the feast, Romeo climbs a wall of the Capulets' property and finds himself: in a courtyard, in an orchard, by the stables or next to a lake?

50. Is Peter, Petruchio or Paris a mute follower of Tybalt?

TWELFTH NIGHT

1. Which amusing character in the play has a fondness for alcohol and is related to Olivia?

2. Which female character is Sebastian's twin?

3. Who leaves at the end of the play, vowing revenge on all those assembled?

4. Does Olivia vow to mourn the death of her brother for one, three, five or seven years?

5. What role does Feste have in Olivia's household?

6. Who starts to wear bright yellow stockings thinking it is what his mistress, Olivia, wants?

7. Which character in the play is the Duke of Illyria?

8. Does Viola, Sebastian or Antonio declare in Act 2, scene 1, 'That danger shall seem sport, and I will go'?

9.   At whose court does Viola first find employment when disguised as a young man?

10. Who is instructed by Orsino to go, 'unfold the passion of my love' to Olivia, only for Olivia to fall for the messenger?

11. Who catches Sir Andrew Aguecheek, Sir Toby Belch and Maria up late at night and threatens to report Maria?

12. When they are getting along well at the start of Act 3, what does Cesario reward Feste with?

13. What is the alternative title of this play?

14. Who tells Malvolio off for lacking patience and declares, 'O, you are sick of self-love'?

15. Who mistakenly attacks Sebastian in Act 4 but has to be saved from further beating by Sir Toby Belch?

16. Who 'proves' Olivia is a fool because she is mourning her dead brother even though she believes his soul is in heaven?

17. What name does Viola take as she disguises herself as a young man?

18. Who gives Sebastian his purse of money and then, when captured by guards mistakenly asks Viola for it back?

19. Does Malvolio find and read the forged love letter to him in Olivia's bedroom, the garden, the cellars or the grand hall?

20. Who does Feste tell Malvolio he is when visiting Malvolio in the dark room?

21. What piece of jewellery does Olivia, via her servants, try to give to Cesario?

22. Maria forges a love letter in her mistress, Olivia's handwriting. Who is the intended target of the trick?

23. Who ends the play singing a song with the chorus, 'For the rain it raineth every day'?

24. Who does Viola fall in love with whilst disguised as a young man: Sir Toby Belch, Antonio or Orsino?

25. At the start of the play, who is Orsino in love with?

26. Can you recall the very first line of the play, a comment about love by Orsino?

27. Who proposes marriage to Sebastian in Act 4?

28. 'To be up after midnight and to go to bed then is early,' declares which character in the play?

29. Who rescues Sebastian from the shipwreck?

30. Is Fabian a servant of Olivia, Orsino or Viola?

31. Who do Sir Toby Belch, Maria and Sir Andrew Aguecheek secretly watch fantasise about being a Count?

32. Who follows Sebastian to the court of Duke Orsino even though he has enemies there?

33. Maria and Sir Toby Belch encourage who to try and win Olivia's hand in marriage?

34. At the start of Act 4, who does Feste think is Cesario and begin an argument with?

35. Who is about to fight Viola disguised as Cesario when Antonio saves her?

36. When checking they are really twins in Act 5, what facial feature does Viola say her brother had on his brow?

37. How many languages does Sir Toby Belch say Sir Andrew Aguecheek can speak: one or two, three or four, five or six or seven or eight?

38. Which character in Act 5 repeats a phrase in Maria's letter and says, 'Some are born great, some achieve greatness, and some have greatness thrown upon them'?

39. Who, surprisingly, marries Maria: Antonio, Duke Orsino or Sir Toby Belch?

40. How old were the twins when their father died?

41. Whose singing voice does Sir Andrew Aguecheek call 'a mellifluous voice' whilst Sir Toby Belch calls it, 'a contagious breath'?

42. Who proposes marriage to Viola in Act 5 of the play?

43. Who exclaims, 'O time! thou must untangle this, not I;/It is too hard a knot for me to untie' after discovering that Olivia is in love with a woman dressed as a man?

44. Is Olivia's female maid called Viola, Maria, Valentine or Thisbe?

45. Is Malvolio, Sebastian, Curio or Feste Olivia's steward?

46. Of whom does Malvolio speak when he says to Olivia, 'I marvel your ladyship takes delight in such a barren rascal'?

47. Who is Feste arguing with when he says, 'Many a good hanging prevents a bad marriage'?

48. Who does Sebastian tell they must separate so that, 'I can bear my evils alone'?

49. What is the name of the lodgings – the same as a large animal – in the south suburbs that Antonio suggests Sebastian stays in?

50. What is the name of the sea captain who survives the shipwreck along with Viola?

AS YOU
LIKE IT

1. What relation are Oliver and Orlando to
   each other?

2. Who hangs love poems to Rosalind in the
   trees of the forest?

3. What is the name of the wrestler Oliver
   hopes will kill Orlando?

4. Which servant offers all his wealth, some five
   hundred crowns, to Orlando?

5. What relation are Celia and Rosalind?

6. What is the name of the court fool who falls
   in love with Audrey?

7. Who wins the wrestling match between
   Charles and Orlando?

8. Who threatens to take the family fortune
   from Oliver unless he finds Orlando?

9. Is Hymen the god of revenge, marriage,
   money or forest creatures?

10. Does Oliver marry Celia, Rosalind, Phebe or Audrey?

11. Who calls Audrey a 'foul slut' to which she replies, 'I am not a slut, though I thank the gods I am foul'?

12. Is Corin a nobleman, a shepherd, a vicar or a soldier?

13. Which character gives the epilogue to the play and states, 'If I were a woman I would kiss as many of you as had beards that pleased me'?

14. Who mournfully speaks to Rosalind in Act 5 saying, 'But, O, how bitter a thing it is to look into happiness through another man's eyes!?'

15. Who brings Oliver and the court news of the overthrow of Duke Senior?

16. To which forest is Duke Senior banished when he is overthrown?

17. Who says that, 'Men are April when they woo, December when they wed'?

18. Who is happy in exile and states, 'Sweet are the uses of adversity …'?

19. What relation to Duke Frederick is Celia?

20. Can you recall the next line from Rosalind after, 'Do you not know I am a woman …'?

21. What item of jewellery does Rosalind give Orlando to wear in Act 1?

22. Is Audrey a noblewoman, a seamstress, a goatherd or a witch?

23. Which shepherd does Silvius tell of his love for the shepherdess, Phebe?

24. Which member of Duke Frederick's court interrupts Celia and Rosalind as they talk about the sport of love in Act 1?

25. Is Dennis a shepherd, a servant, a spy or a cook?

26. Who says to Phebe, 'I pray you do not fall in love with me/For I am falser than vows made in wine …'?

27. Who insists on 'rustic revelry' before he and the others leave the forest?

28. Which member of Duke Frederick's court does Rosalind suggest should accompany the women on their travels to the Forest of Arden?

29. Which gloomy lord and friend of Duke Senior claims that he, 'can suck melancholy out of a song as a weasel sucks eggs'?

30. Which woman falls in love with Ganymede but eventually marries Silvius?

31. Who brings news that Duke Frederick is raising an army to attack Duke Senior?

32. In Act 4, Oliver is saved by Orlando from what creature?

33. When Touchstone asks William how old he is, what is William's reply?

34. What name does Celia take on leaving Duke Frederick's court?

35. Can you recall the line from the play that follows: 'All the world's a stage …'?

36. What happens to Frederick at the end of the play?

37. Who falls in love with Rosalind, the daughter of Duke Senior?

38. What is Sir Oliver Martext's occupation?

39. Who pretends to be a vicar in the pretend marriage of 'Ganymede' and Orlando?

40. Can you name both men who try to woo Audrey?

41. Which woman accompanies Rosalind as she escapes to the Forest of Arden?

42. Duke Frederick banishes which of his nieces because he suspects her of possible treason?

43. Who offers his estate to Orlando in Act 5?

44. How many marriages occur in Act 5 of the play?

45. Who is the youngest son of Sir Rowland?

46. Le Beau tells Celia and Rosalind of a wrestling match between Charles and the eldest of three brothers. What bones in this man's body did Charles break?

47. Who is the oldest of the shepherds and shepherdesses: Corin, Phebe or Silvius?

48. Who disguises herself as a youth called Ganymede?

49. According to Jaques, one man during his life may play many parts but how many ages does he go through?

50. Which pair of lovers from ancient history does Rosalind talk about, who became the subject of a later play by Shakespeare?

MUCH ADO ABOUT NOTHING

1. Which war hero falls in love with a character called Hero?

2. Who urges Don Pedro to get married, saying, 'Prince, thou art sad, get thee a wife'?

3. What is the name of the Governor of Messina, beginning with the letter L?

4. Can you name the couple who plan to get Benedick and Beatrice to fall in love with each other?

5. Which character is the Prince of Arragon?

6. Is Dogberry, Balthasar or Conrade the constable who investigates Don John?

7. Who says, 'Let every eye negotiate for itself,/And trust no agent; for beauty is a witch …'?

8. What is the name of Leonato's daughter?

9. Which figure flees from Messina, but news at the very end of the play tells of his capture?

10. Who is called 'this rotten orange' on the day of her wedding?

11. With which man does Beatrice frequently bicker and argue?

12. On Hero and Claudio's wedding day, who tells Leonato that Hero has met with a 'ruffian' who, 'Confess'd the vile encounters they have had/A thousand times in secret'?

13. How many ducats does Don John plan to pay Borachio for his deception that makes others think Hero is unfaithful?

14. When Leonato tells Friar Francis that there is no impediment to Hero's marriage, who says, 'O, what men dare do!'?

15. Who challenges Claudio to a duel in Act 5?

16. What is the name of the adopted niece of Leonato?

17. Who says there is a 'kind of merry war' between Benedick and Beatrice?

18. For at least how long does Don Pedro say he will stay with Leonato?

19. Who, on getting married at the end of the play, speaks its last words: 'Strike up, pipers'?

20. Which two followers of Don John are arrested by Dogberry?

21. Who offers to disguise himself as Claudio to help woo Hero for Claudio?

22. In which act does Hero reveal to Benedick and the others that she is not dead?

23. Who is the illegitimate brother of Don Pedro?

24. Who asks Borachio and Conrade if they serve God and on hearing their reply, says, 'Write down, that they hope they serve God: and write God first; for God defend but God should go before such villains!'?

25. Which companion of Don John's makes love to Margaret in a trick designed to make Claudio think Hero is being unfaithful?

26. Who is called 'Lady Disdain' by Benedick?

27. Can you name either of Hero's gentle-women?

28. Who says to Beatrice, 'But it is certain I am loved of all ladies, only you excepted'?

29. Is *Much Ado About Nothing* considered one of Shakespeare's tragedies, comedies or romances?

30. Does the play take place in Padua, Messina or Venice?

31. Does Hero faint, run away or commit suicide after she is accused at her wedding by Claudio?

32. Who is Antonio's 'daughter', in reality?

33. In which act do Beatrice and Benedick admit their love for each other?

34. Who accuses Hero of lechery on her wedding day?

35. Antonio says that grieving more inside than one shows to the outside world is what distinguishes men from: women, children or animals?

36. Can you recall the line which follows, 'I pray thee, cease thy counsel,/Which falls into mine ears as profitless as …'?

37. Apart from telling the whole city of Hero's innocence and marrying Antonio's daughter, what is Claudio's other punishment?

38. Is Antonio's brother: Don John, Borachio, Leonato or Dogberry?

39. Who tells Don Pedro in Act 1 that, '… I will live a bachelor.'?

40. What is the name of the friar who believes that Hero is innocent of the charges uttered by Claudio on their wedding day?

41. Does Benedick come from Rome, Padua, Venice or Florence?

42. Who pretends to be Claudio at a masked ball but remains silent, forcing Hero to say, 'So you walk softly, and look sweetly, and say nothing'?

43. Who believes it would be best if Hero died, saying, 'Death is the fairest cover for her shame …'?

44. From which Italian city does Claudio come?

45. Who comes up with the idea of pretending Hero is actually dead to get Claudio to reconsider his accusations?

46. What half-completed documents found in both Beatrice and Benedick's rooms do Hero and Claudio make public near the end of the play?

47. What was the first line of Claudio's epitaph to Hero?

48. What line follows Hero saying, 'If it proves so, then loving goes by haps'?

49. Who is deputy to the chief of police: Conrad, Verges or Antonio?

50. Can you recall Antonio's next line after, 'Content yourself. God knows, I loved my niece ...'?

OTHELLO

1. Who is the Moor of Venice: Iago, Desdemona or Othello?

2. Of what island is Montano the Governor?

3. What is Othello's profession: doctor, lawyer, soldier or governor?

4. Which two characters both kill their own wives in the play?

5. Who is Othello's wife?

6. In which act of the play does Othello first collapse into a trance or fit due to his jealousy?

7. Who in Act 3 says, 'O, beware, my lord, of jealousy!/It is the green-eyed monster, which doth mock/The meat it feeds on ...'?

8. At the end of the play, does Iago escape, is he executed or is he left in the hands of Montano?

9. Who stabs Roderigo to death: Othello, Cassio or Iago?

10. Who accuses Othello of using magic to win the love of Desdemona?

11. Does Ludovico, Iago, Cassio or Roderigo tell Othello that he has been ordered to return from Cyprus to Venice?

12. Is Gratiano, Ludovico or Roderigo the brother of Brabanzio?

13. Who, in a fit of jealous rage, kills Desdemona?

14. What is the first item Desdemona receives as a gift from Othello: a necklace, a gold bracelet, a handkerchief or a rare book?

15. How is Desdemona killed: by being poisoned, drowned, smothered or stabbed?

16. Who was promoted above Iago by Othello?

17. Who does Othello call a demon and a devil in Act 5, Scene 2?

18. Which female character tells Othello that he has killed, '… the sweetest innocent/That e'er did lift up eye'?

19. Who despairs once Othello and Desdemona marry but is told to keep hoping by Iago?

20. When Iago seeks to get Cassio drunk in Act 2, he sings a song about an English king whose 'breeches cost him but a crown'. What was the name of the king?

21. As what kind of monster does Iago describe jealousy?

22. Who finds Desdemona's handkerchief on the floor and gives it to Iago to use as part of his plot to make Othello jealous?

23. To whom does Othello say, 'I love thee,/ But never more be officer of mine'?

24. Does the weather, a witch's curse or Othello's fleet destroy the enemy ships?

25. Did a Turk, an Egyptian, a Venetian or a German give Othello's mother the handkerchief?

26. What is the full name of Othello's lieutenant?

27. What is the name of the officer intent on revenge on Othello at the start of the play for not being promoted?

28. Which female character is given Desdemona's handkerchief to copy by Cassio?

29. Does the Clown, Iago or Roderigo mock Cassio's choice of musicians in Act 3?

30. Against which force is Othello leading the Venetian army?

31. Which female character's father is Brabantio?

32. Which character says she will 'play the swan,/And die in music …'?

33. Who does Ludovico say is Lord Governor at the end of the play?

34. Is Roderigo, Montano or Cassio in love with Desdemona?

35. Who says that he has 'looked upon the world for four times seven years, and since I could distinguish betwixt a benefit and an injury, I never found man that knew how to love himself'?

36. Is Gratiano, Cassio or Othello grateful that Desdemona's father is dead so that he does not have to suffer the pain of her murder?

37. Who is Brabantio addressing when he says, 'O thou foul thief! Where hast thou stowed my daughter?'

38. Who is impressed with Othello, saying that, 'I have serv'd him, and the man commands/ Like a full soldier'?

39. Who insists that a fight about to begin doesn't happen, saying, '... keep up your bright swords, for the dew will rust them'?

40. Can you name both characters who go to Brabantio to tell him of Othello eloping with Desdemona?

41. Who sings a song starting, 'Willow, willow, willow' as she dies?

42. After getting drunk who does Cassio fight with and wound in Act 2: Iago, Graziano, Montano or Bianca?

43. Who says, '... guiltiness I know not; but yet I feel fear'?

44. Which character is plied with alcohol by Iago although he should not drink much?

45. What fruit is part of the pattern on Desdemona's handkerchief?

46. How does Othello die: by taking poison, by hanging himself or by stabbing himself?

47. What part of Cassio is seriously injured in the fight in Act 5: his leg, his arm or his head?

48. What is the title of the man who summons Othello and orders him to Cyprus?

49. What is the name of Iago's wife?

50. Which character's last words are, 'Killing my self, to die upon a kiss.'?

MACBETH

1. Who kills Macbeth?

2. Whose ghost terrifies Macbeth at supper in Macbeth's castle?

3. What title does Macbeth have at the start of the book?

4. Who laments, 'The Thane of Fife had a wife; where is she now? What, will these hands ne'er be clean?'?

5. Who is the last person Macbeth kills?

6. In the witches' prophecy, what is the name of the wood that will have to move before Macbeth is defeated?

7. Who declares that he will, '… fight till from my bones my flesh be hacked'?

8. Is Macbeth's castle at Aberdeen, Dundee, Inverness or Edinburgh?

9. In Act 4, when Macbeth meets the witches again, who does the first apparition warn Macbeth to beware of?

10. Who urges Macbeth to 'screw your courage to the sticking-place'?

11. What is the name of Banquo's son?

12. How many murderers does Macbeth hire to kill Banquo and his son?

13. What is the name of the Thane of Fife?

14. What line follows the witches' chant of 'Double, double toil and trouble …'?

15. About what does Macbeth say to himself that, 'If it were done when 'tis done, then 'twere well/It were done quickly …'?

16. Which characters chant, 'Fair is foul, and foul is fair:/Hover through the fog and filthy air'?

17. Who believes Macbeth is, 'too full o' th' the milk of human kindness' to perform dastardly deeds?

18. Who escapes when Banquo is killed by murderers?

19. The second apparition that warns Macbeth in Act 4 takes the form of: a goat's head, a skeleton or a bloodied child?

20. Who is with Macbeth as they return from battle and are met for the first time by the three witches?

21. Who is hailed as King of Scotland at the end of the play?

22. What is the last line Macduff's son says as he is murdered?

23. What three things does the porter tell Macduff that alcohol provokes?

24. Who smears King Duncan's guards with blood to make it appear they murdered the king?

25. When the captain describes the battle to King Duncan as being evenly matched, what analogy does he use about swimming?

26. Which son of Duncan tests Macduff's loyalty to Scotland in Act 4?

27. King Duncan hears reports of which invading nation's forces being beaten by those of Macbeth?

28. A doctor watches Lady Macbeth sleepwalking and imagining her hands are covered in what substance?

29. A gentlewoman and a doctor watch which character at the start of Act 5?

30. '… for none of woman born/Shall harm Macbeth' is spoken by Lady Macbeth, Hecate or the Second Apparition?

31. Which monkey's blood was used to cool the ingredients of the witches' cauldron to make the charm 'firm and good'?

32. Does the first, second or third witch hail Macbeth, 'that shalt be king hereafter'?

33. Can you name both of King Duncan's sons?

34. What is the name of the queen of the witches, beginning with the letter H?

35. Were a Turk's, a Tartar's or a Moor's lips part of the ingredients in the witches' cauldron?

36. In Act 4, Macbeth learns that Macduff has fled to which country?

37. Which friend does Macbeth come across whilst on his way to kill King Duncan?

38. Who discovers the dead body of King Duncan?

39. Who says to Macbeth, 'Your face, my thane, is as a book where men/May read strange matters ...?

40. Which one of the following is not an ingredient in the witches' cauldron: viper snake fillet, a dog's tongue, a wolf's tooth or gall of goat?

41. Does Lennox, the Porter, Caithness or Lady Macbeth tell Macbeth that Macduff has fled to England?

42. Who dies first: Macbeth, Young Siward or Lady Macbeth?

43. Was Sweno a servant of Macbeth, a king of Norway or the son of Macduff?

44. At the start of the play, after the first witch asks, 'When shall we three meet again?' does the second witch reply, 'that will be ere the set of sun', 'when Macbeth hath won' or, 'when the hurly-burly's done'?

45. Who turns out not to have been, 'of woman born': Malcolm, Banquo, Macduff or Fleance?

46. Whose sons did the witches predict would become kings in the future?

47. At the end of the play, is Malcolm to be crowned at Glamis, Edinburgh, Birnam Wood or Scone?

48. Who speaks to Macbeth moments before Duncan's body is discovered saying, 'The night has been unruly. Where we lay/Our chimneys were blown down …'?

49. What rank is the soldier who reports Macbeth's vanquishing of the rebel Macdonald to King Duncan?

50. Does Duncan's son, Donalbain, flee to England, Ireland, France or Wales?

THE
MERCHANT
OF VENICE

1. Of what religious faith is Shylock?

2. Although Shylock may be entitled to a pound of flesh, what must he not spill a drop of?

3. Where does Portia live: Athens, Venice or Belmont?

4. Which friend of Antonio's seeks to woo Portia?

5. Portia's father devised a test to see who should marry her. How many chests does it involve?

6. Which character says, 'If you prick us do we not bleed? If you tickle us do we not laugh?' to Salerio and Solanio?

7. Does Launcelot, Antonio or Lorenzo say to Jessica, '… the sins of the father are to be laid upon the children; therefore I promise you I fear you'?

8. Whose ships are believed to have 'miscarried' resulting in him being unable to pay off his debts?

9. Who falls in love with Portia's maid?

10. Is the Prince of Morocco, the Prince of Arragon or the Neapolitan prince the fifth suitor of Portia?

11. Who disguises herself as Balthazar, a young doctor of law?

12. Beginning with the letter L, what is the name of Shylock's dead wife whom he misses greatly?

13. What piece of jewellery does Portia give Bassanio?

14. Who asks at the court of the Duke of Venice, 'Do all men kill the things they do not love?'?

15. Who does Tubal say spent fourscore ducats at a sitting in Genoa?

16. Who was first Shylock's servant before becoming a servant of Bassanio?

17. Each of the chests used in the test of Portia's suitors was made from a different material. Can you recall two of them?

18. Which couple is Shylock forced to leave all his wealth to?

19. Who accompanies Bassanio to Belmont as Bassanio plans to win Portia's hand in marriage?

20. The Neapolitan prince who is one of Portia's suitors talks about only one subject. Can you recall what?

21. Which casket does Bassanio choose when faced with the test?

22. Which one of Antonio's friends becomes Nerissa's suitor?

23. What does Jessica disguise herself as in order to leave her father's household and be with the person she is in love with?

24. Is Lorenzo a Jew, Christian, Muslim or a non-believer?

25. Who says, 'The quality of mercy is not strained,/It droppeth as the gentle rain from heaven'?

26. Tubal comes to visit Shylock in Venice, but from what city did he travel?

27. What is the name, beginning with the letter F, of the English baron who tries to woo Portia?

28. According to Tubal, did Jessica trade Shylock's most valuable jewel for a coach and horses, a villa in Padua or a monkey?

29. Does Bellario, an expert in law and Portia's cousin, live in Rome, Padua, Pisa or Naples?

30. In whose service is Launcelot Gobbo at the start of the play?

31. Who warns Bassanio to take his time over the choice of caskets, saying, 'I pray you tarry; pause a day or two/Before you hazard, for in choosing wrong/I lose your company'?

32. How many ducats does Shylock lend Antonio: 100, 300, 1000 or 3000?

33. Who speaks the last line of the play: Portia, Shylock, Gratiano or Antonio?

34. Which prince fears that Portia will not like him because of the dark complexion of his skin?

35. Is the majority of the play in prose or verse?

36. When Portia and Shylock argue the law surrounding Shylock's bond, who is head of the court and makes the final decision?

37. What is the first line of the scroll found inside the gold casket by the Prince of Morocco?

38. How many months does Antonio arrange for his loan with Shylock to last?

39. What does Shylock demand of Antonio should he fail to repay the loan?

40. Which woman tells Lorenzo that she is, 'never merry when I hear sweet music'?

41. What is the name of Jessica's father?

42. At the end of the play how many of Antonio's ships, thought lost, does Portia say have actually reached harbour?

43. What is inside the lead casket opened by Bassanio?

44. Which character is forced to convert to Christianity near the end of the play?

45. Against which Venice merchant does Shylock harbour a longstanding grudge?

46. Who gives away a ring to a clerk at the Venice court only to discover that the clerk was really Nerissa?

47. Who does Lorenzo run away from Venice with?

48. When Portia disguises herself as a doctor of law what servant's name does she take as an alias?

49. Which one of the following is not a servant of Portia's: Stephano, Salerio, Balthasar?

50. Who does Shylock maintain has '… laughed at my losses, mocked at my gains, scorned my nation, thwarted my bargains'?

A MIDSUMMER NIGHT'S DREAM

1. Who is king of the fairies: Oberon, Demetrius or Theseus?

2. Who does Demetrius marry at the end of the play?

3. Which fairy falls in love with Bottom?

4. In which Greek city do Theseus and Hippolyta marry?

5. Who accuses Demetrius of hurting Lysander, saying, 'Out, dog! Out, cur! Thou driv'st me past the bounds/Of maiden's patience'?

6. How many weddings take place at the end of the play?

7. What sort of creatures are Peaseblossom, Mustardseed and Cobweb?

8. What is the name of the play performed by the artisans after the weddings?

9. Robin Goodfellow is better known as which character in the play?

10. Philostrate is Master of the Revels, in the court of which character?

11. Which one of the four lovers says, 'Are you sure/That we are awake? It seems to me/That yet we sleep, we dream'?

12. Is Starveling a weaver, tailor or carpenter?

13. Who instructs Puck to make a fog to separate the four quarrelling lovers in the forest?

14. Which character does Puck give the head of an ass?

15. Do Theseus and the others wake the lovers when they enter the wood on a hunt, on a search party for them or when battling the Amazons?

16. Which relative of Lysander's do he and Hermia intend to flee to in order to marry?

17. Who says of Bottom that, 'Thou art wise as thou art beautiful'?

18. Who is the Queen of the Amazons, beginning with the letter H?

19. What is the name of the Duke of Athens in this play?

20. Who plays the role of Pyramus in the play: Bottom, Quince, Starveling or Snout?

21. How do Thisbe and Pyramus die in the play: by stabbing, poisoning or hanging themselves?

22. At the start of the play, how many days are there to go before Theseus and Hippolyta marry?

23. Which of the men plays the part of the moon in the play put on for Theseus's wedding?

24. At the start of the story, who is Helena in love with?

25. What is Bottom's first name?

26. Is Snout a tailor, soldier, tinker or spy?

27. Is Flute, Snout, Bottom or Snug a bellows-mender?

28. Who does Lysander hear say the words, 'O hell! To choose love with another's eye'?

29. Who, in Act 2, chides Oberon for possibly loving Hippolyta, saying, 'Your buskin'd mistress and your warrior love,/To Theseus must be wedded'?

30. Who does Oberon order to bring him a flower from Cupid?

31. Shortly after the clock strikes which hour does Theseus say is fairy time?

32. Hermia has two suitors when she arrives at the palace of Theseus. Can you name either of them?

33. Who tricks Demetrius and Lysander by using their own voices to stop them fighting?

34. When Oberon removes the spell on Titania, who is she shocked to find is lying in her arms?

35. Does Hermia's father want her to marry Lysander, Demetrius, Theseus or Starveling?

36. When the others who are rehearsing their play see Bottom with the head of an ass, do they all laugh, faint or flee?

37. Under Athenian law at this time, who could tell a girl who she should marry?

38. Hermia is given three choices, one of which is to marry Demetrius. Can you recall either of the others?

39. Who objects to playing the role of the lady, Thisbe, but eventually takes it on?

40. What sort of craftsman is Quince?

41. In the play to celebrate Theseus and Hippolyta's wedding, what creature scares Thisbe off from her meeting at the tomb?

42. Who exclaims, 'O Helen, goddess, nymph, perfect, divine!'?

43. In the forest, who does Lysander fall in love with: Titania, Hermia or Helena?

44. Which of the characters planning to perform a play for Theseus is afraid that if the lion appeared too realistic it would frighten the ladies in the audience?

45. Who warns Theseus that the play is not suitable for him to watch, saying, 'It is not for you. I have heard it over,/And it is nothing, nothing in the world'?

46. Who, after watching Lysander in the forest, exclaims, 'Lord, what fools these mortals be!'?

47. Does Theseus, Oberon or Lysander say in Act 1 that, 'The course of true love never did run smooth'?

48. Is Bottom a potter, a carpenter, a tailor or a weaver?

49. Who gives a soliloquy at the end of the play including the lines: 'If we shadows have offended,/Think but this, and all is mended,/That you have but slumb'red here …'?

50. Which pair of characters quarrel in the forest over an orphan boy?

THE COMEDIES

1. In which Shakespeare comedy do you find Silvia, Julia and the Duke of Milan?

2. In *Troilus and Cressida* does Ajax, Priam or Achilles finally kill Hector?

3. In *The Comedy of Errors*, must Egeon pay 10, 100 or 1000 marks, otherwise he will die?

4. From which country does Don Adriano de Armado come, in *Love's Labour's Lost*?

5. In *All's Well That Ends Well*, who gets to choose any husband she wishes after helping to improve the King of France's health?

6. In *Love's Labour's Lost*, the King asks his Lords to renounce women and commit themselves to how many years of study?

7. In *The Two Gentlemen of Verona*, can you name one of Sylvia's three suitors?

8. In *Measure For Measure*, what is the name of Claudio's sister who is a novice in a sisterhood of nuns?

9. What is the name of the kingdom in *Love's Labour's Lost* where Ferdinand reigns?

10. In *The Two Gentlemen of Verona*, what is the name of Launce's pet dog: Rover, Crab, Speed or Lucius?

11. Who asks Isabella to marry at the end of *Measure For Measure* saying, 'What's mine is yours and what is yours is mine.'?

12. Who, in *Love's Labour's Lost*, visits Navarre to repay debts from France?

13. Can you name two of the three suitors for Anne Page in *The Merry Wives of Windsor*?

14. Who, in *Troilus and Cressida*, is Priam's daughter?

15. In *All's Well That Ends Well*, does Helena fall in love with Bertram, Lafew, Rynaldo or the Duke of Florence?

16. Vincentio in *Measure For Measure* had been Duke of which city for fourteen years?

17. In *Troilus and Cressida*, is Priam, Agamemnon or Ulysses the Commander in Chief of the Greek forces?

18. To whom does Cressida give a love token, annoying Troilus?

19. In *The Comedy of Errors*, what is the name of both twins, beginning with the letter A?

20. In *Measure For Measure*, is Elbow an executioner, a priest, a constable or a clown?

21. In *The Two Gentlemen of Verona*, who arranges for the outlaws to be pardoned by the Duke near the play's end?

22. Which husband of one of the wives Falstaff tries to seduce in *The Merry Wives of Windsor* takes the alias, Brook?

23. Is Lavatch, Mariana or Parolles, the bad tempered clown in *All's Well That Ends Well*?

24. Who is described as, 'a most notable coward, an infinite and endless liar' in *All's Well That Ends Well*?

25. In *The Comedy of Errors*, was Aemilia, Luciana, Adriana or Nell the name of Egeon's wife, from whom he was parted after the shipwreck?

26. Who are the two gentlemen of Verona in the play of the same name?

27. Which male French doctor in *The Merry Wives of Windsor* ends up unwittingly marrying a boy?

28. Who in *Measure For Measure* is condemned to death for 'fornication' and getting his lover pregnant?

29. In *All's Well That Ends Well*, do Bertram and Parolles go to fight in Spain, France, England or Italy?

30. In *Measure For Measure* who confesses and believes he should be put to death but is instructed to marry Mariana instead?

31. In which Shakespeare comedy would you find the Page and the Ford families as well as Mistress Quickly, Peter Simple and characters called Shallow and Slender?

32. In *The Comedy of Errors*, what is the name of both twins, beginning with the letter D?

33. Pistol and Nim reveal whose plans to seduce the wives in *The Merry Wives of Windsor*?

34. In *All's Well That Ends Well*, who does Helen replace in bed to trick her husband, Bertram?

35. Is Bertram's title, in *All's Well That Ends Well*, the Duke of Florence, the King of France or the Count of Rossillion?

36. In *The Two Gentlemen of Verona*, who disguises herself as a boy called Sebastian to spy on Proteus?

37. Who, in *Troilus and Cressida*, says, 'Why tell you me of moderation?/The grief is fine, full, perfect that I taste': Cressida, Ajax, Achilles or Troilus?

38. In *Love's Labour's Lost*, who gives the wrong love letters to the wrong ladies with comic effect?

39. In *Measure For Measure*, whose head does Vincentio pretend he holds?

40. In *Love's Labour's Lost* does Rosaline, Katherine or Maria promise herself to Berowne if he can hold his biting tongue and wit?

THE TRAGEDIES

1. In which Act of *Timon of Athens* does Timon hand a large amount of gold to Alcibiades?

2. After being banished, Coriolanus turns up in Antium disguised as: a beggar, a priest, a clown or a woman?

3. Does Lucius, Titus Andronicus or Aaron become the emperor of Rome?

4. In *Coriolanus*, who says, 'Now put your shields before your hearts, and fight/With hearts more proof than shields'?

5. In *Julius Caesar*, is Portia the wife of Mark Antony, Caesar, Marcus Brutus or Caius Ligarius?

6. Does Timon of Athens discover a hoard of gold in a lake, an old hut or a forest?

7. In *Titus Andronicus*, Alarbus is killed as a sacrifice in Act 1; but who was his mother?

8. Who is the Roman emperor in *Titus Andronicus* whose name contains the name of a planet?

9. Who was bailed out of jail by Timon yet when wealthy refuses to help Timon?

10. Can you name either of Titus Andronicus's children, both beginning with the letter L?

11. About Brutus, Mark Antony, Cassius or Cicero does Julius Caesar remark that he has 'a lean and hungry look'?

12. In *Titus Andronicus*, Lavinia turns down the offer to become Roman empress because she is in love with which other character?

13. Is Aufidius, Nicanor, Cominus or Menenius a Volscian general who orders Coriolanus's murder?

14. In *Julius Caesar*, can you complete the short warning to Caesar uttered in Act 1 by the Soothsayer, which begins, 'Beware …'?

15. Is Volumnia, Valeria or Virgilia Coriolanus's mother?

16. Can you name either of the characters Titus Andronicus kills and has their blood and bones made into pasties eaten by their mother?

17. In *Coriolanus* what creature does Young Martius tear to pieces with his teeth?

18. Two characters identified only by their occupations, approach Timon to ask to serve him in Act 5. Can you recall either of them?

19. Which of his servants does Timon tell off when he learns he has no money left?

20. Which ally of Coriolanus says in Act 5, 'I neither care for th' world nor your general'?

21. What is the name of the clothing Coriolanus wears in front of the citizens before he is made consul?

22. To which former enemy did Coriolanus offer his 'revengeful services' to help conquer Rome?

23. Who is Julius Caesar's wife: Portia, Calpurnia, Titinius or Cinna?

24. When penniless, Timon invites the friends who refuse to help him to one last feast. What two items are on the plates served at the feast?

25. In *Titus Andronicus*, who is the Queen of the Goths?

26. In *Timon of Athens*, whose epitaph is translated by Alcibiades, part of which reads, 'Here lies a wretched corse [corpse], Of wretched soul bereft ...'?

27. In *Coriolanus*, Volumnia boasts that her son has added two new war wounds to those he already has. Do they number 3, 7, 14 or 25?

28. What is the name of the Moor who is the lover of the Queen of the Goths in *Titus Andronicus*?

29. Who do Chiron and Demetrius rape in *Titus Andronicus*?

30. In the harrowing killings at the end of *Titus Andronicus*, can you put the following deaths in the order they occur: Titus, Saturninas, Tamora, Chiron?

31. In *Coriolanus*, are the Greeks, Volsces, Turks or Vandals the enemy that fights Rome?

32. What is the profession of Alcibiades in *Timon of Athens*: soldier, priest, lawyer or doctor?

33. By what other name is Coriolanus known?

34. In *Timon of Athens*, which general is banished from Athens but returns to attack the city?

35. Can you recall Julius Caesar's famous last words as he is stabbed by a number of Romans, including Brutus?

36. Throughout the play, how many of Titus Andronicus's sons are killed?

37. In *Julius Caesar*, who says to Cassius, 'Let's be sacrificers, but not butchers, Caius' when trying to save Mark Antony from being killed as well as Caesar?

38. Is Valeria, Volumnia or Virgilia the wife of Coriolanus?

39. In *Titus Andronicus*, which character is buried up to his neck and starved?

40. In *Timon of Athens*, does Apemantus, Ventidius or Timon say, 'It grieves me to see so many men dip their meat in one man's blood'?

THE
ROMANCES

1. In *The Two Noble Kinsmen*, who is the Queen of the Amazons, beginning with the letter H?

2. Is Hermione a shepherd girl, the Queen of Sicily or a Bohemian princess in *The Winter's Tale*?

3. Is *Cymbeline*, *Pericles* or *The Winter's Tale* set in Ancient Britain?

4. Does Pericles vow to never cut his hair or wash his face when he believes his wife, his daughter or his son has died?

5. Who dies in a horse riding accident in *The Two Noble Kinsmen*?

6. In *The Winter's Tale* is Leontes the King of Verona, Tunis, France or Sicily?

7. Just as she is about to be killed by Leonine, do soldiers, pirates, a group of nuns or an unruly mob take Marina away?

8. In *Cymbeline*, what piece of jewellery of Imogen's does Iachimo steal from her whilst she is sleeping?

9. What is the name of Pericles's and Thaisa's daughter, born at sea during a storm?

10. Which king tries to poison the King of Bohemia in *The Winter's Tale*?

11. In *The Two Noble Kinsmen*, when the two princes duel, which one wins?

12. Who does Iachimo convince that his wife has not been faithful in the play, *Cymbeline*?

13. Thaisa devotes herself to a goddess of chastity when parted from Pericles, but is the goddess's name Ophelia, Hippolyta or Diana?

14. Which place struggling with famine welcomes Pericles as a hero for bringing ships laden with food?

15. In *The Two Noble Kinsmen*, who is the Duke of Athens, beginning with the letter T, who attacks Thebes and imprisons Arcite and Palamon?

16. In Act 3 of *Cymbeline*, Imogen receives a letter from her husband directing her to travel to which country?

17. What creature attacks and kills Antigonus in *The Winter's Tale*?

18. Who does Leontes promise he will never marry without her permission?

19. In which of Shakespeare's romances does a character called John Gower act as a narrator?

20. In *The Two Noble Kinsmen*, which of the Princes of Thebes does the Gaoler's Daughter fall in love with?

21. In *The Winter's Tale*, is Polixenes the King of Sicily, Bohemia or Naples?

22. Does Leontes mourn the loss of his wife for sixteen weeks, months or years?

23. In *Pericles*, what do suitors for the King of Antioch's daughter have to do to win her hand, facing death if they do not?

24. Which member of King Cymbeline's family takes the disguise of a boy called Fidele?

25. Guiderius kills which stepson of Cymbeline's and drops his head into the ocean, 'to tell the fishes he's the queen's son'?

26. In *Cymbeline*, who does Leontes believe has slept with his wife: Camillo, Polixenes or Autolycus?

27. Had Belarius been banished from Cymbeline's court two, five, ten or twenty years before the play's action?

28. In *Pericles*, what is the name of the king who sleeps with his own daughter?

29. At the end of *The Winter's Tale*, a statue of which character miraculously comes to life?

30. What is the name of Cymbeline's daughter?

31. The King of Antioch hires a villain called Thaliart to kill which character in *Pericles*?

32. In *The Two Noble Kinsmen*, who, mourning the loss of his cousin, says, 'Emilia,/To buy you, I have lost what's dearest to me …'?

33. Posthumus Leonatus is the adopted son of which character in *Cymbeline*?

34. After plotting to kill Pericles's daughter, how are Dionyza and Cleon killed by an angry mob?

35. Can you name either of the two noble kinsmen in the play of the same name?

36. In *The Winter's Tale*, is Perdita brought up by a merchant, a sailor, a shepherd or a baker?

37. Does Posthumus Leonatus order Philario, Pisanio or Cornelius to kill Imogen in Cymbeline?

38. Over which young woman do the two Princes of Thebes clash in *The Two Noble Kinsmen*?

39. In *The Winter's Tale*, Florizel falls in love with Imogen but who forbids them to marry, believing Imogen is a commoner?

40. Is Pericles a prince, lord, king or commoner at the start of the play?

THE HISTORY PLAYS

1.   What is the name of the girl born to Henry VIII and Anne Boleyn?

2.   Does a monk, a knight or his wife kill King John using poison?

3.   Can you complete the line from *Henry IV Part 1* which reads, 'The better part of valour is ...'?

4.   In *Henry IV Part 1* of whom does Prince Harry say, 'Thou art so fat-witted with drinking of old sack ...'?

5.   Is Edward III's wife, Victoria, Philippa or Gwendoline?

6.   In *Richard II*, does John of Gaunt, Hotspur or Thomas Mowbray accuse Richard II of destroying 'this royal throne of kings'?

7.   Which French town is captured by Edward III, who orders the execution of six of its inhabitants: Calais, Poitiers or Angers?

8. In *Henry VI*, who is the English hero
    captured by the French who is so feared
    that archers guard him as he sleeps?

9. Queen Margaret and Lord Clifford murder
    which Duke in the play, *Henry VI Part 3*?

10. In which Shakespeare play does an English
    king try to woo the Countess of Salisbury?

11. In *Edward III*, does King Edward, the Black
    Prince or the Earl of Audley capture the
    French king, King John?

12. In which Shakespeare history play do Lord
    Talbot and his son both die together?

13. Can you add the missing word to complete
    the line from the play, *Henry VI Part 3*:
    'The smallest ____ will turn, being
    trodden on'?

14. In the play *King John*, is Pandolf an
    ambassador from France or the Pope?

15. Which character says near the start of *Henry
    VI Part 1* that, 'I am by birth a shepherd's
    daughter,/My wit untrained in any kind of
    art'?

16. The play *Henry VIII* has the subtitle, *Measure for Measure*, *All Is True*, *The Monarch of Windsor* or *A Man And His Wives*?

17. Can you add the missing word to complete the line from *Henry VI Part 3*: 'The first thing we do, let's kill all the _____'?

18. At the end of *Henry IV Part 2*, are Falstaff and his friends: rewarded with riches by the new king, pardoned for their actions or sent to a naval prison?

19. King Edward IV and Lady Elizabeth Grey marry in which play: *Richard II*, *Henry V* or *Henry VI Part 3*?

20. 'Tell him the crown that he usurps is mine,/And where he sets his foot he ought to kneel' are lines from *Edward III*, *Richard II* or *Henry VI Part 1*?

21. In *Henry VI Part 1*, Joan helps the French break the English siege around which French town: Calais, Orleans or Paris?

22. In *Henry VIII*, Cardinal Wolsey tries to stop Henry VIII marrying which of his wives?

23. Does the line, 'He will give the devil his due' come from *Richard II, Edward III* or *Henry IV Part 1*?

24. When he leads a revolt in *Henry VI Part 2*, does Jack Cade pretend to be Cardinal Beaufort, the Duke of Suffolk or Sir John Mortimer?

25. Can you fill in the word missing from the end of these lines from *Henry IV Part 1*: 'If all the year were playing holidays,/ To sport would be as tedious as to ____'?

26. Do the rival armies in *King John* fight over the French town of Auxerre, Angiers, Reims or Lyons?

27. Who is Richard II's queen?

28. In *King John* which character is the illegitimate son of Richard the Lionheart who supports King John throughout much of the play?

29. Which one of the following is not a character in *Henry VI Part 2*: the Duke of Buckingham, Thomas Horner, King Ferdinand, Queen Margaret?

30. Is Arthur, Richard or James supported by the King of France as the rightful heir to the throne in *King John*?

31. In *Henry VI Part 1*, which French heroine is burned at the stake?

32. In *Henry IV Part 2*, who complains about Falstaff that, 'He hath eaten me out of house and home'?

33. 'Uneasy lies the head that wears a crown' are words uttered by which king in one of Shakespeare's history plays?

34. 'A man can die but once,' is a phrase uttered by Feeble, in *Henry VIII*, *King John* or *Henry IV Part 2*?

35. Which comic character is a large knight who likes to eat and drink, and appears in *Henry IV Parts 1* and *2*, *Henry V* and *The Merry Wives of Windsor*?

36. In *Henry VI Part 1*, who is told by Joan of Arc, 'thy hour is not yet come' when they meet on the battlefield?

37. Which king does Sir Piers of Exton murder in Pomfret Castle?

38. In *Henry VI Part 2*, what is the name of Henry VI's wife who plots and kills the Duke of Gloucester?

39. Many of Shakespeare's history plays deal with the war between the houses of York and Lancaster. What flowery name is often given to this conflict?

40. In *Henry IV Part 1*, Henry Percy is a rival of Prince Harry and the same age, but is he better known as Falstaff, Hotspur or Shallow?

THE NARRATIVE POEMS AND SONNETS

1. In *Venus and Adonis*, who promises to kiss Venus at first but then refuses?

2. Most of Sonnets 127 to 152 are addressed to or are about a woman with what colour hair?

3. Sonnets 153 and 154 are about which god of love?

4. How many lines are there in a sonnet?

5. In which of Shakespeare's poems is there a character called Brutus?

6. In Sonnet 73, does Shakespeare call darkness and night, 'the envelope of black', 'Death's second self' or 'that blackened shroud'?

7. In *Venus and Adonis*, which creature kills Adonis?

8. *In Sonnets to Sundry Notes of Music*, which month of the year does Shakespeare say is the month of love?

9. Who says in *The Rape of Lucrece*, 'As from this cold flint I enforced this fire,/So Lucrece must I force to my desire'?

10. In *Venus and Adonis*, what colour is the flower that appears from the ground where Adonis's body had lain?

11. What is the last word of Sonnet 139, 'Yet do not so, but since I am near slain,/Kill me outright with looks, and rid my ____'?

12. In which poem do two birds mate to preserve one of the bird's beauty?

13. In *The Rape of Lucrece*, what is the name of the man who rapes Lucrece?

14. 'Mine enemy was strong, my poor self weak' is a line from *The Rape of Lucrece*, *Venus and Adonis* or *The Phoenix and the Turtle*?

15. In which Shakespeare poem is the body of a woman who committed suicide carried through Rome?

16. Does the famous line, 'Shall I compare thee to a summer's day?' come from Sonnet 18, Sonnet 30 or Sonnet 144?

17. 'From fairest creatures we desire increase,' is the opening line of Sonnet 1, 18, 34 or 49?

18. Can you complete the last line of Sonnet 154, 'Love's fire heats water, …'?

19. In which of Shakespeare's poems does a man kiss a woman who has fainted, only for him to die later?

20. Does Lucrece's father, husband or sister manage to catch the name of the rapist from her dying breaths?

21. Which season of the year is described in Sonnet 73?

22. In *Venus and Adonis*, who says, 'Fie, no more of love! The sun doth burn my face. I must remove'?

23. In *The Rape of Lucrece*, what is the name of Lucrece's husband: Collatine, Antonio or Lucio?

24. Which of Shakespeare's poems is only 67 lines long?

25. Is Adonis out hunting, farming or getting drunk in a tavern the first time he meets Venus?

26. In *A Lover's Complaint*, does a man or a woman throw love tokens into a river near the poem's start?

27. 'Lo! in the orient when the gracious light …' is the opening line of: Sonnet 3, Sonnet 7 or Sonnet 23?

28. In Sonnet 18, 'Rough winds do shake …' what?

29. Can you recall the line that follows, 'Shall I compare thee to a summer's day?'?

30. In *The Phoenix and the Turtle*, what type of bird acts as a priest near the start of the poem?

31. 'Not marble, nor the gilded monuments/ Of princes, shall outlive this powerful rhyme' is the start of Sonnet 38, *A Lover's Complaint* or Sonnet 55?

32. What sort of creature is the turtle in *The Phoenix and the Turtle*?

33. Does a shepherd, a cattle herder or a goatherd join the upset woman by the river bank in *A Lover's Complaint*?

34. In *The Phoenix and the Turtle*, is 'Threnos' a priest, a bird or a funeral song?

35. Venus describes Adonis as how many times fairer than herself?

36. How does Lucrece die – by poisoning, drowning, strangling or stabbing herself?

37. 'That thou art blamed shall not be thy defect' is the opening line of Sonnet 18, Sonnet 70 or Sonnet 132?

38. In which poem does a women lament falling for a man so beautiful that both men and women find him irresistible?

39. Who was Lucrece's father: Tarquin, Brutus or Lucretius?

40. What is the title of the collection of poems including sonnets first published in 1599: *The Passionate Pilgrim*, *The First Folio* or *The Phoenix and the Turtle*?

ANSWERS

1. Stratford-upon-Avon
2. Comedies, Histories and Romances
3. *A Midsummer Night's Dream*
4. *King Lear*
5. Three
6. *Hamlet*
7. Rome
8. Sonnet
9. *Hamlet*
10. *King Lear*

11. *Macbeth*
12. *The Merchant of Venice*
13. Ancient Rome
14. *The Merchant of Venice*
15. A poem
16. *Love's Labour's Lost*
17. Isabella
18. The Trojan War
19. *Twelfth Night*
20. *Romeo and Juliet*

21. Hands, tongue
22. *Julius Caesar*
23. Denmark
24. *A Midsummer Night's Dream*
25. *Cymbeline*

26. Mark Antony
27. *Twelfth Night*
28. *Macbeth*
29. *Othello*
30. Friar Ludowick

31. *The Tempest*
32. *The Comedy of Errors*
33. *Henry IV Part II*
34. Falstaff
35. Helen
36. Brutus
37. *Macbeth*
38. Henry IV
39. Rosaline, Maria, Katharine
40. Anne Page

41. *Coriolanus*
42. Dromio
43. *Hamlet*
44. Her father
45. *Pericles*
46. Ephesus and Syracuse
47. *Measure for Measure*
48. Theseus
49. '… run smooth'
50. Proteus

SHAKESPEARE'S LIFE AND TIMES

1. The Globe
2. John
3. 16th century
4. Anne Hathaway
5. Eleven
6. Women
7. *First Folio*
8. Queen Elizabeth I
9. *Henry VIII*
10. London

11. Groundlings
12. Seven
13. St George's Day
14. The Master of the Revels
15. One
16. Shakespeare himself
17. After his death
18. The Earl of Southampton
19. 1997
20. His mother

21. King James I
22. The Comfort
23. Glove maker
24. Over 1500 people
25. Queen Elizabeth I
26. Thomas

27. 1599
28. An outbreak of plague
29. Over 35
30. *The Two Noble Kinsmen*

31. A flag
32. A theatre company
33. The Royal Shakespeare Company
34. Holy Trinity Church, Stratford
35. The King's Men
36. *Venus and Adonis*
37. *Richard III*
38. Eight years older
39. *Macbeth, Othello, King Lear*
40. *As You Like It*

41. On his gravestone
42. Red
43. Where actors changed costume
44. King James I
45. The Rose
46. Hamnet and Judith
47. Banquo
48. The pit
49. 154 sonnets
50. New Place

KING LEAR

1. Three
2. Goneril
3. Cordelia
4. Goneril
5. The Earl of Gloucester
6. Edmund
7. Cordelia
8. Regan
9. Edgar
10. Edgar

11. King Lear
12. Goneril
13. Edgar
14. The Fool
15. King of France, Duke of Burgundy
16. Poor Tom (Edgar)
17. Act 4
18. Six days
19. Lear
20. Edgar

21. 25
22. France
23. Albany
24. Oswald
25. Caius (Kent)
26. Cordelia

27. 48
28. Poor Tom
29. Goneril
30. Edgar

31. Goneril
32. The Earl of Gloucester
33. Dover
34. The Duke of Burgundy
35. The Earl of Kent
36. Goneril
37. Goneril and Regan
38. 'Lest it see more, prevent it./Out, vile jelly!'
39. Edmund
40. '… crack your cheeks'

41. Lear
42. The Duke of Cornwall
43. Cordelia
44. Over 80
45. '… it is to have a thankless child.'
46. Oswald
47. Goneril
48. The Earl of Kent
49. 'Speak less than thou knowest,'
50. King Lear

HENRY V

1. Chorus
2. Agincourt
3. Harry
4. 60,000
5. Bardolph
6. MacMorris
7. Katherine
8. Act 2
9. Charles VI
10. Southampton

11. Lord Scrope
12. The Duke of Clarence
13. Three
14. Henry
15. Queen Isabel
16. The Duke of Exeter's
17. Harfleur
18. France
19. The Bishop of Ely
20. Scottish

21. The Duke of York
22. Sir John Falstaff
23. Northumberland
24. King Henry V
25. Harfleur
26. Pistol

27. Archbishop of Canterbury
28. Fluellen
29. The Duke of Bedford
30. Bardolph

31. English
32. The Duke of Exeter
33. "… England and Saint George!"
34. Ireland
35. The Boar's Head Tavern
36. Alice
37. Sir John Falstaff
38. Nim and Bardolph
39. Crowns (coins)
40. A leek

41. '… His bleeding sword 'twixt England and fair France.'
42. Pistol
43. Montjoy
44. Southampton
45. Five to one
46. Pistol
47. Gloves
48. Sir Thomas Grey
49. Tennis balls
50. King Henry V

THE TAMING OF THE SHREW

1. Petruchio
2. Bianca
3. Sunday
4. Tranio, Biondello
5. Lucentio
6. Petruchio
7. Cardmaker
8. Three
9. Fifteen
10. Hortensio

11. Christopher Sly
12. A lute
13. Padua
14. Petruchio
15. Music tutor
16. Gremio
17. Ten times
18. Cambio
19. Venice
20. Kate

21. Lucentio
22. Kate
23. Petruchio
24. Kate
25. Tranio
26. Hortensio
27. Her Latin tutor

28. 'If I be waspish, best beware my sting.'
29. Tranio (disguised as and on behalf of Lucentio)
30. Vincentio

31. The moon
32. Hortensio
33. Hunting
34. Kate
35. Lucentio's father
36. He does not let her eat.
37. Lucentio
38. 'Why she's a devil, a devil, the devil's dam.'
39. Grumio
40. Petruchio

41. Baptista (her father)
42. Kate
43. Petruchio
44. '... but eat and drink as friends'
45. Kate
46. Christopher Sly
47. Grumio
48. Vincentio
49. Bianca
50. Wife

THE TEMPEST

1. A storm
2. Prospero
3. A slave
4. A spirit that appears in the masque
5. Miranda
6. Prospero
7. Caliban
8. Prospero
9. Cold porridge
10. Caliban

11. Ferdinand
12. Stephano
13. Gonzalo
14. His books
15. Stephano, Caliban and Trinculo
16. Prospero
17. Caliban
18. Miranda
19. Prospero
20. Stefano

21. 'And what strength I have's mine own'
22. Ferdinand
23. Carry wood

24. Tunis
25. Hounds
26. Miranda
27. Antonio
28. Gonzalo
29. A banquet
30. Antonio

31. Ariel
32. Gonzalo
33. Twelve years
34. Sleeping
35. Antonio
36. A witch
37. Stefano
38. Trinculo
39. Ferdinand
40. Chess

41. Claribel
42. A circle
43. Prospero
44. Alonso
45. Gonzalo
46. Miranda
47. Ariel
48. Ferdinand
49. Caliban
50. Lions

ANTONY AND CLEOPATRA

1. Egypt
2. Three
3. Octavia
4. To avenge the death of his father
5. Eros
6. Charmian
7. Pompey
8. Triumvir
9. Syria
10. Figs

11. Cleopatra
12. Alexas
13. Octavius
14. Lepidus
15. Octavius Caesar
16. Mark Antony
17. Iras, Charmian
18. Arm and chest
19. Octavius Caesar
20. Scarus

21. He falls on his own sword
22. A clown
23. Athens
24. Cleopatra
25. '... nor custom stale/ Her infinite variety.'

26. A pearl
27. Philo
28. Caesar's
29. Agrippa
30. Mark Antony

31. Treasurer
32. He sends Ventidius
33. Act 4
34. Cleopatra
35. Drunk
36. 60
37. Charmian
38. Proculeius
39. Enobarbus
40. Cleopatra

41. Menas
42. Cleopatra's
43. Syria
44. Octavius Caesar
45. Antony
46. Octavia
47. Crying
48. Fulvia
49. Octavius Caesar
50. Sorrow at Cleopatra's dying

HAMLET

1. Prince of Denmark
2. Drowning
3. '... that is the question,'
4. Osric
5. Horatio
6. Norway
7. Polonius
8. Elsinore
9. Francisco, Barnardo, Marcellus
10. Wittenberg

11. Laertes
12. The court jester
13. 'The slings and arrows of outrageous fortune,'
14. 'Wherein I'll catch the conscience of the King.'
15. Laertes's
16. 'The Mouse-trap'
17. Gertrude
18. Claudius
19. Rosencrantz
20. To die

21. His ear
22. Laertes
23. Julius Caesar
24. Fortinbras

25. '... forty thousand brothers'
26. Claudius
27. France
28. His father
29. Hamlet
30. Laertes

31. Gertrude
32. Claudius
33. Laertes
34. Claudius
35. '... the state of Denmark.'
36. Rosencrantz, Guildenstern
37. Yorick
38. Ophelia's
39. Polonius
40. England

41. Claudius
42. Ophelia
43. The ghost
44. 'Why wouldst thou be a breeder of sinners?'
45. Gertrude (his mother)
46. Queen Gertrude
47. Fortinbras
48. The ghost of King Hamlet
49. Polonius
50. Laertes

RICHARD III

1. '... My kingdom for a horse!'
2. They are brothers
3. Two
4. Canterbury
5. Pomfret
6. Edward IV
7. His arm
8. Sir James Tyrrel
9. Brakenbury
10. Edward, Prince of Wales (son of Henry VI)

11. Lady Anne
12. Queen Margaret
13. Edward and Richard
14. Lady Anne
15. Henry, Earl of Richmond
16. Catesby
17. Baynard's Castle
18. Prince Edward
19. Bishop of Ely
20. Anne

21. Queen Margaret
22. '... Do never live long'
23. Richard Gloucester
24. Lord Hastings
25. France

26. Bosworth Field
27. King Richard III
28. A supporter
29. Elizabeth
30. Catesby

31. Duke of Clarence
32. Eagles
33. An archbishop
34. The Duke of Clarence's
35. The Tower of London
36. George, Duke of Clarence
37. Derby
38. A boar
39. Lord Stanley's
40. One of Henry Tudor's followers

41. Cowards
42. '... made glorious summer by this son of York'
43. Lady Anne
44. Three
45. King Edward IV
46. Queen Elizabeth
47. The Duchess of York
48. Queen Elizabeth
49. York
50. Thomas Rotherham

ANSWERS

ROMEO AND JULIET

1. Montague
2. Verona
3. Romeo
4. Tybalt
5. Thursday
6. Peter
7. Friar Laurence
8. '... with a kiss I die'
9. Juliet
10. Act 1

11. Balthasar
12. Juliet
13. Mantua
14. 'But soft! What light through yonder window breaks?'
15. Juliet
16. Tybalt's
17. At the very end of the play
18. Paris
19. The Prince of Verona
20. 'Deny thy father and refuse thy name'

21. Capulet
22. Tybalt
23. Rosaline

24. Montague
25. Juliet's nurse
26. Mercutio
27. Thirteen
28. Friar John
29. Romeo
30. Sampson, Gregory

31. The Montagues
32. Friar Laurence
33. Juliet's nurse
34. Tybalt
35. Capulet's wife
36. Queen Mab
37. Paris
38. Two years
39. The Prince of Verona
40. Cousin

41. Stabbing herself
42. Mercutio
43. Romeo
44. Juliet's nurse
45. The Prince of Verona
46. Benvolio
47. Juliet's nurse
48. Friar Laurence
49. In an orchard
50. Petruchio

TWELFTH NIGHT

1. Sir Toby Belch
2. Viola
3. Malvolio
4. Seven years
5. A clown
6. Malvolio
7. Orsino
8. Antonio
9. Duke Orsino's
10. Viola (Cesario)

11. Malvolio
12. Money (coins)
13. *What You Will*
14. Olivia
15. Sir Andrew Aguecheek
16. Feste
17. Cesario
18. Antonio
19. The garden
20. Sir Topas

21. A ring
22. Malvolio
23. Feste
24. Orsino
25. Olivia

26. 'If music be the food of love, play on'
27. Olivia
28. Sir Toby Belch
29. Antonio
30. Olivia

31. Malvolio
32. Antonio
33. Sir Andrew Aguecheek
34. Sebastian
35. Sir Andrew Aguecheek
36. A mole
37. Three or four
38. Feste
39. Sir Toby Belch
40. Thirteen

41. Feste's
42. Orsino
43. Viola (Cesario)
44. Maria
45. Malvolio
46. Feste
47. Maria
48. Antonio
49. The Elephant
50. Antonio

AS YOU LIKE IT

1. Brothers
2. Orlando
3. Charles
4. Adam
5. Cousins
6. Touchstone
7. Orlando
8. Duke Frederick
9. Marriage
10. Celia

11. Touchstone
12. A shepherd
13. Rosalind
14. Orlando
15. Charles
16. The Forest of Arden
17. Rosalind
18. Duke Senior
19. His daughter
20. 'When I think, I must speak.'

21. A chain
22. A goatherd
23. Corin
24. Touchstone
25. A servant
26. Rosalind

27. Duke Senior
28. Touchstone, the clown
29. Jaques
30. Phebe

31. Jaques de Boys
32. A lioness
33. Twenty five years old
34. Aliena
35. 'And all the men and women merely players'
36. He becomes a religious hermit
37. Orlando
38. He is a vicar
39. Aliena (Celia)
40. William and Touchstone

41. Celia
42. Rosalind
43. Oliver
44. Four
45. Orlando
46. Ribs
47. Corin
48. Rosalind
49. Seven
50. Troilus and Cressida

MUCH ADO ABOUT NOTHING

1. Claudio
2. Benedick
3. Leonato
4. Claudio, Hero
5. Don Pedro
6. Dogberry
7. Claudio
8. Hero
9. Don John
10. Hero

11. Benedick
12. Don Pedro
13. 1000 ducats
14. Claudio
15. Benedick
16. Beatrice
17. Leonato
18. At least a month
19. Benedick
20. Conrade and Borachio

21. Don Pedro
22. Act 5
23. Don John
24. Dogberry
25. Borachio
26. Beatrice
27. Margaret, Ursula
28. Benedick

29. One of the comedies
30. Messina

31. She faints
32. Hero
33. Act 4
34. Claudio
35. Children
36. '… water in a sieve.'
37. To compose and read an epitaph for Hero at her tomb
38. Leonato
39. Benedick
40. Friar Francis

41. Padua
42. Don Pedro
43. Leonato
44. Florence
45. Friar Francis
46. Love poems
47. 'Done to death by slanderous tongues'
48. 'Some Cupid kills with arrows, some with traps'
49. Verges
50. 'And she is dead, slandered to death by villains …'

OTHELLO

1. Othello
2. Cyprus
3. Soldier
4. Iago and Othello
5. Desdemona
6. Act 4
7. Iago
8. He is left in the hands of Montano
9. Othello
10. Brabantio

11. Ludovico
12. Gratiano
13. Othello
14. A handkerchief
15. By being smothered
16. Cassio
17. Iago
18. Emilia
19. Roderigo
20. King Stephen

21. A green-eyed monster
22. Emilia
23. Cassio
24. The weather
25. An Egyptian

26. Michael Cassio
27. Iago
28. Bianca
29. The Clown
30. The Turks

31. Desdemona's
32. Emilia
33. Cassio
34. Roderigo
35. Iago
36. Gratiano
37. Othello
38. Montano
39. Othello
40. Iago and Roderigo

41. Emilia
42. Montano
43. Desdemona
44. Cassio
45. Strawberry
46. By stabbing himself
47. His leg
48. The Duke of Venice
49. Emilia
50. Othello's

MACBETH

1. Macduff
2. Banquo's
3. Thane of Glamis
4. Lady Macbeth
5. Young Siward
6. Great Birnam Wood
7. Macbeth
8. Inverness
9. Macduff
10. Lady Macbeth

11. Fleance
12. Three
13. Macduff
14. 'Fire burn, and cauldron bubble'
15. The murder of King Duncan
16. The three witches
17. Lady Macbeth
18. Fleance
19. A bloodied child
20. Banquo

21. Malcolm
22. 'He has kill'd me, mother./Run away I pray you.'
23. Nose-painting, sleep and urine
24. Lady Macbeth

25. 'As two spent swimmers that do cling together/And choke their art.'
26. Malcolm
27. Norway's
28. Blood
29. Lady Macbeth
30. The Second Apparition

31. Baboon's blood
32. The third witch
33. Malcolm and Donalbain
34. Hecate
35. A Tartar's lips
36. England
37. Banquo
38. Macduff
39. Lady Macbeth
40. A viper snake fillet

41. Lennox
42. Lady Macbeth
43. A king of Norway
44. 'when the hurlyburly's done'
45. Macduff
46. Banquo's sons
47. Scone
48. Lennox
49. Captain
50. Ireland

ANSWERS

THE MERCHANT OF VENICE

1. He is a Jew
2. Blood
3. Belmont
4. Bassanio
5. Three
6. Shylock
7. Launcelot
8. Antonio's
9. Gratiano
10. The Prince of Morocco

11. Portia
12. Leah
13. A ring
14. Bassanio
15. Jessica
16. Launcelot
17. Gold, silver, lead
18. Jessica and Lorenzo
19. Gratiano
20. Horses

21. The lead casket
22. Gratiano
23. A boy
24. Christian
25. Portia

26. Genoa
27. Falconbridge
28. A monkey
29. Padua
30. Shylock's

31. Portia
32. 3000 ducats
33. Gratiano
34. The Prince of Morocco
35. Prose
36. The Duke of Venice
37. 'All that glisters is not gold'
38. Three months
39. A pound of flesh
40. Jessica

41. Shylock
42. Three
43. A portrait of Portia
44. Shylock
45. Antonio
46. Gratiano
47. Jessica
48. Balthasar
49. Salerio
50. Antonio

A MIDSUMMER NIGHT'S DREAM

1. Oberon
2. Helena
3. Titania
4. Athens
5. Hermia
6. Three
7. Fairies
8. 'Pyramus and Thisbe'
9. Puck
10. Theseus

11. Demetrius
12. A tailor
13. Oberon
14. Bottom
15. On a hunt
16. His aunt
17. Titania
18. Hippolyta
19. Theseus
20. Bottom

21. By stabbing themselves
22. Four
23. Starveling
24. Demetrius
25. Nick
26. A tinker

27. Flute
28. Hermia
29. Titania
30. Puck

31. Midnight
32. Lysander, Demetrius
33. Puck
34. Bottom
35. Demetrius
36. Flee
37. Her father
38. To become a nun, or to face death
39. Flute
40. A carpenter

41. A lion
42. Demetrius
43. Helena
44. Bottom
45. Philostrate
46. Puck
47. Lysander
48. A weaver
49. Puck
50. Oberon and Titania

The Comedies

1. *The Two Gentlemen of Verona*
2. Achilles
3. 1000 marks
4. Spain
5. Helena
6. Three years
7. Valentine, Thurio, Proteus
8. Isabella
9. Navarre
10. Crab

11. Vincentio, the Duke
12. The Princess of France
13. Fenton, Slender and Dr Caius
14. Cassandra
15. Bertram
16. Vienna
17. Agamemnon
18. Diomedes
19. Antipholus
20. A constable

21. Valentine
22. Frank Ford
23. Lavatch
24. Parolles
25. Aemilia
26. Valentine, Proteus
27. Dr Caius
28. Claudio
29. Italy
30. Angelo

31. *The Merry Wives of Windsor*
32. Dromio
33. Falstaff's
34. Diana
35. The Count of Rossillion
36. Julia
37. Cressida
38. Costard
39. Claudio's
40. Rosaline

THE TRAGEDIES

1. Act 4
2. A beggar
3. Lucius
4. Caius Martius
5. Marcus Brutus
6. A forest
7. Tamora
8. Saturninus
9. Ventidius
10. Lucius, Lavinia

11. Cassius
12. Bassianus
13. Aufidius
14. '... the ides of March'
15. Volumnia
16. Chiron, Demetrius
17. Butterflies
18. The Poet and the Painter
19. Flavius
20. Menenius

21. The gown of humility
22. Aufidius
23. Calpurnia
24. Warm water, stones
25. Tamora
26. Timon's
27. 25
28. Aaron
29. Lavinia
30. Chiron, Tamora, Titus, the Emperor

31. The Volsces
32. Soldier
33. Caius Martius
34. Alcibiades
35. 'Et tu Brute? Then fall Caesar!'
36. Three
37. Brutus
38. Virgilia
39. Aaron
40. Apemantus

THE ROMANCES

1. Hippolyta
2. The Queen of Sicily
3. *Cymbeline*
4. His daughter
5. Arcite
6. Sicily
7. Pirates
8. A bracelet
9. Marina
10. Leontes, the King of Sicily

11. Arcite
12. Posthumus Leonatus
13. Diana
14. Tarsus
15. Theseus
16. Wales
17. A bear
18. Paulina
19. *Pericles*
20. Palamon

21. Bohemia
22. Sixteen years
23. Answer a riddle correctly
24. Imogen
25. Cloten
26. Polixenes
27. 20 years earlier
28. Antiochus
29. Hermione
30. Imogen

31. Pericles
32. Palamon
33. King Cymbeline
34. They are burned to death
35. Palamon, Arcite
36. A shepherd
37. Pisanio
38. Emilia
39. Polixenes
40. A prince

THE HISTORY PLAYS

1. Elizabeth
2. A monk
3. '... discretion'
4. Falstaff
5. Philippa
6. John of Gaunt
7. Calais
8. Talbot
9. The Duke of York
10. *Edward III*

11. The Black Prince
12. *Henry VI Part 1*
13. 'worm'
14. The Pope
15. Joan
16. *All Is True*
17. 'lawyers'
18. Sent to a naval prison
19. *Henry VI Part 3*
20. *Edward III*

21. Orleans
22. Anne Boleyn
23. *Henry IV Part 1*
24. Sir John Mortimer
25. 'work'
26. Angiers
27. Queen Isabel
28. Philip the Bastard
29. King Ferdinand
30. Arthur

31. Joan (of Arc)
32. Mistress Quickly
33. King Henry IV
34. *Henry IV Part 2*
35. Falstaff
36. Talbot
37. King Richard II
38. Margaret
39. The Wars of the Roses
40. Hotspur

NARRATIVE POEMS AND SONNETS

1. Adonis
2. Black
3. Cupid
4. Fourteen
5. *The Rape of Lucrece*
6. 'Death's second self'
7. A wild boar
8. May
9. Tarquin
10. Purple

11. 'pain'
12. *The Phoenix and the Turtle*
13. Tarquin
14. *The Rape of Lucrece*
15. *The Rape of Lucrece*
16. Sonnet 18
17. Sonnet 1
18. '... water cools not love'
19. *Venus and Adonis*
20. Her husband

21. Autumn
22. Adonis
23. Collatine
24. *The Phoenix and the Turtle*
25. Hunting
26. A woman
27. Sonnet 7
28. '... the darling buds of May.'
29. 'Thou art more lovely and more temperate.'
30. A swan

31. Sonnet 55
32. A bird (a turtle dove)
33. A cattle herder
34. A funeral song
35. Thrice (three times)
36. By stabbing herself
37. Sonnet 70
38. *A Lover's Complaint*
39. Lucretius
40. *The Passionate Pilgrim*